THE CULTURE CLUB

71870

THE CULTURE CLUB
Crisis in the Arts
BRYAN APPLEYARD

faber and faber
LONDON · BOSTON

First published in 1984
by Faber and Faber Limited
3 Queen Square London WC1N 3AU
Printed in Great Britain by
Redwood Burn Limited
Trowbridge Wiltshire
All rights reserved

© *Bryan Appleyard, 1984*

British Library Cataloguing in Publication Data

Appleyard, Bryan
The culture club
1. Arts and society—Great Britain
I. Title
700'.941   NX180.S6

ISBN 0–571–13385–1
ISBN 0–571–13279–0 (Pbk)

Library of Congress Data has been applied for

FOR MY FATHER

The Insider
Beckett, Camus, Chomsky, Einstein, Eliot,
Fanon, Freud, Gandhi, Guevara (Che), Joyce,
Jung, Kafka, Lawrence, Laing, Le Corbusier,
Lenin, Lévi-Strauss, Lukács, Mailer, Marcuse,
Marx, McLuhan, Orwell, Popper, Proust,
Reich, Russell, Weber, Wittgenstein, Yeats.
Just reciting the names made me feel better.

C. Vita-Finzi, entry for the New Statesman
*competition (1975) in which competitors were
asked for the first paragraphs of novels the Arts
Council had subsidized them not to write*

The committee gained the impression that the
arts had reached an impasse.

*Eighth report from the Education, Science and
Arts Committee of the House of Commons,*
Public and Private Funding of the Arts *(1982)*

CONTENTS

1

THE PROBLEM

Lord Goodman's face, the chin just level with the surface of his massive desk, takes on a prophetic look: 'The tendency towards less civilization and more cretinous behaviour has undoubtedly been increased by a few millimetres.'

From behind a Perrier and a desk consisting of a thick sheet of glass perched uneasily on top of a square pillar made of the same concrete as the exterior of the National Theatre, Sir Peter Hall contemplates the end of the 'Whither Britain?' school of drama: 'I think it's over, and I think the people working in it think it's over, and I don't know what's going to happen next.'

At 48 Sir Roy Strong thinks that life is finite, and he has no intention of helping to keep the Arts Council treadmill turning.

Stephen Bayley runs the Boilerhouse Project, a gallery of contemporary design. His office is cool and bleak with an uncharacteristically gaudy rug to subdue the brittle acoustics. 'At some point,' he muses, 'the visual arts just alienated themselves from the public. That's the story of modern art. It's been a futile exercise ever since. If anything interesting is happening in painting, it hasn't come to my attention.'

Melvyn Bragg occupies a corner of the London Weekend Television tower on the South Bank. Also keen on Perrier, he tends to flop into strategically placed sofas. 'I'm part of the retreat from the moral high ground,' he admits.

In the midst of a seminar at the Institute of

Contemporary Arts Malcolm Bradbury stares at a point on the far wall several feet over the heads of the audience of friends, literary agents, publishers and writers. He speaks of the exciting, new 'defamiliarization of the familiar' in the renaissance of British fiction.

For Lord Goodman something faintly distasteful seems to be going on. Sir Peter discerns an aesthetic hiatus, while Sir Roy is dismayed by a glum bureaucracy. Bayley, the one newcomer, thinks the old fine arts are played out; Bragg is searching for a point from which he need retreat no further; Bradbury is busily constructing a renaissance.

For all these mandarins there seems to be a problem. Few are content to speak optimistically or with pride in what has been, and what is going to be, achieved. Instead there is a nagging doubt, an air of ennui and irritation. It arises partly from the battles they have fought and are reluctant to fight again and partly from a sense that the tide has turned against them in some indefinable way. They are no longer members of a confident priesthood officiating at the shrine of art with the support of an enthusiastic and aspiring congregation. The muttering from the pews can no longer be ignored. Perhaps the faithful are about to go elsewhere, leaving this largely 1960s-based generation of clergy with an empty church. Bayley is the odd man out. For him the fine art faith is dead: long live design.

Various theories are put forward to account for the unease—money, the Tory Government, philistinism, VAT.... But really there seems simply to be a kind of weariness at yet again having to defend the citadel of art from something threatening 'out there'. Sir Claus Moser, chairman of the Royal Opera House, when asked why public money should be invested in the arts, replied with an air of deep fatigue: 'Only in this country is this question still asked.' So, rather than go through all the rows and justifications again, the mandarins fall back on an appeal to common sense. Surely, they think, along with Dame Ninette de Valois, nobody would think of getting rid of the Royal Ballet now? It would be madness.

Perhaps. But torpor or inattention could do the job equally well. For the real disease is a kind of obesity. It is characterized by a loss of impetus and energy, an inability to concentrate and a feeling that although enough has been consumed, more needs to be acquired.

The vast paraphernalia of associations, obligations and commercial imperatives which had been hung on the slender notion of art have left it gasping for breath. But the post-war growth in the total market—combined with the cosy, liberal belief that art is good, Governments should do good, therefore Governments should fund the arts—have forced the pace. More and more has been demanded of art, and only now is it becoming clear that it cannot deliver.

The prize in this post-war race for growth is evaporating at the very moment that it is being won. For art is edgy, dynamic, seldom satisfied with generalizations and constantly obliged to question its own being. Neither the modern marketplace nor government money shares any of those qualities. Instead there is an oddly vacant air, first identified in its embryonic form by Iris Murdoch in 1961: 'The Welfare State has come about as a result, largely, of socialist thinking and socialist endeavour. It has seemed to bring a certain struggle to an end; and with that ending has come a certain lassitude about fundamentals.'*

In the arts that lassitude is beyond politics, economics, aesthetics and psychology; it is an uneasy synthesis of them all. It was apparent in last year's National Theatre

*Iris Murdoch, 'Against Dryness: a Polemical Sketch', *Encounter*, 1961; reprinted in Malcolm Bradbury (ed.), *The Novel Today*, London/ Glasgow, Fontana, 1982, pp. 25–6.

production of *You Can't Take it with You*. The curtain
rose on an insanely elaborate set, which the audience at
once applauded just as pop audiences applaud familiar
songs: *at the beginning*. What energy there was had gone
into the set, a grim, pedantic, mimetic reconstruction of
the world for our delectation, an aesthetic impulse of
grinding inconsequence, a loading of the dice against
change and imagination. One member of the Royal
Shakespeare Company spoke to me proudly of the little
tricks of recognition that the company played with its
audience, the delicate in-house jokes that everybody
loves. Miss Murdoch wrote in the same essay: 'For the
hard idea of truth we have substituted a facile idea of
sincerity.'

Outside the directly subsidized arts there is a frenetic
atmosphere. The film industry, in partnership with
television, is in the midst of an economic, though
only sporadically creative, upturn; literature has become obsessed with prizes; architecture aspires to a
new vernacular consisting of a glib pastiche of the
old. Lugubriously an aesthetic movement is being
constructed from convulsions in the marketplace.
Variety and quantity are taken to indicate an artistic
renewal, the latest incarnation of the other great liberal
belief that art is good, more art is better.

Clearly, in this climate the idea that something is
fundamentally wrong will not go down well with the
mandarins. They prefer to see the arts as too diffuse, too
plural to be submitted to one analysis, a single critique.
The plurality is, after all, one of its key liberal virtues. It
allows for evolutionary change and the free exchange of
ideas and talent. In this they are helped by the way in
which the arts are reported. Critics review; reporters
interview, plug shows and produce stories about money
problems or the latest pile of bricks at the Tate Gallery;
Arts Council rows erupt and subside; viewing figures

rise and fall; the British film industry is reborn; somebody dies.... They are all relayed back to the public as disparate, contingent events. In the midst of the real world of flying bullets and the SDP, the arts should be just a happy, bubbling, frothy mass which flings up books, shows, rows and stars for our occasional diversion. And so they are, but they are also bound together by hidden, mysterious forces—ideas, misconceptions and ambitions which are seldom discussed and which do yield to a single type of analysis. An arts world view can have a meaning, though it may be a sad one.

But world views, in art as elsewhere, are out of fashion. What was once called holism is disparaged as inhuman. Difficulties are always local. That way, of course, you do not have to think, merely to solve and move on to the next crisis. In fact, thinking is really out. Thinking is what the planners did when they built tower blocks. Thinking is what those nasty conceptual artists did when they stuck typewritten messages on gallery walls. Thinking is what the great modernist masters did, and they were the ones who caused all the trouble in the first place by being foreign and obscure. And we are all post- or rather anti-modernists now.

Problem-solving is the name of the game. How to live with less money, how to sell tickets, how to get the real kittens to stay on the desk in the first act at the National. Faced with such living immediacy, such bread-and-butter posers, the artist and his managers can only find the fundamentals embarrassingly gauche, unchic, redolent of late-night undergraduate conversations.

'Good God, are you asking everybody that?' exclaimed Sir Roy Strong when I inquired what he thought art was. It makes it difficult to do a job if you have to sit down and redefine it every day. But, alas, that is one of the conditions of art; it is obliged to be awkward about its means and its nature, to reinvent itself every morning.

Modernism, this century's one clear artistic signature, was about the relocation of the aesthetic centre in the notion of form. It questioned the nature of expression and the validity of any sense of artistic self. Meaning could no longer be detached and carried away from the work intact, to be digested at leisure with the aid of the Sunday papers. But so often post-war British art has floundered on as if nothing had happened. This is not simply a question of aesthetic insularity; it takes in the institutions and organizations we have founded to meet the demands of the market and the welfare evangelists.

These elements all point in one direction, not because money or lack of it dictates the quality of art, not because of historical determinism and not because politics are the only truth, but because the arts industry has been constructed on a single conception. It may not be sincerely believed—indeed, Lord Goodman describes it as a 'benign illusion'—but it is the unspoken rule that the arts are good and that people should get more of them. Furthermore, they will want more of them once they see how good they are. Behind this there is the assumption that there is something called 'art', which is a state of grace in which people in the arts dwell. That the end justifies the means of grubbing around for cash or fighting committees of dullards is unquestioned. And they would be right to ask no questions if the grubbing and the fighting were done with a certain passion, if occasionally the end products were self-evidently and self-consciously works of genius. Time will tell, of course, but it is difficult to believe it will tell us very much.

The arts, as we so confidently call them, are in need of change, in need of a turning away from sub- sidies, sponsorship, show business—even, if necessary, audiences. They lack a vision, with all that word's attendant associations of megalomania, unreality and stubbornness. The necessity for change is my subject. It involves the practical and functioning idea of art in Britain today—the province of the Culture Club, with its select and secretive committee and its shifting body of members, which has expropriated the idea of art and is now at a loss to know what to do with it.

The Club's problem all along was that it had been formed to do something which by common consent is impossible—to plan for art. 'For if any definite conclusions emerge ...' wrote T. S. Eliot, 'one of them is surely this, that culture is the one thing we cannot deliberately aim at.'* Sir William Rees-Mogg, chairman of the Arts Council, has made the same point: 'What we can't do is say we want to have great art and get it.' Yet over the past forty years more people have been wanting to give it and more wanting to get it. The problem with the resultant blizzard of activity is that it generates its own apparent justification. Inevitably, it comes to be felt that the mere fact of the expenditure of so much energy must mean that the product is finally worthwhile. Indeed, it is obliged to bear its worthiness like a badge— to be about discernibly 'big' issues like politics or the plight of modern man.

It should be made clear at this point that I am discussing art—not crafts, not amateur dramatics, not racially determined polemic, not collective reassurance, not communal creativity. It is the notion of art as a definably different quality over and above the pinnacle of mere skill or talent on which the whole edifice of the industry, commercial and subsidized, is based. This notion is present as an aspiration, a sanctification or simply a qualification for a grant. Without it the whole idea of 'worth' or 'value' is called in question. And yet as Gerald Graff puts it in 'The Myth of the Postmodernist

---

*T. S. Eliot, *Notes towards the Definition of Culture,* London, Faber & Faber, 1983, p. 19.

Breakthrough': 'For the last two centuries, Western aesthetic speculation was engaged in a tightrope act in which the significance which must be ascribed to art in order to justify its importance has had to be eliminated from art in order to guarantee its authenticity.'*

This seemingly remote paradox is, in reality, at the heart of the problem. On the one hand, art has been worrying itself out of existence for the last two hundred years. On the other hand, secularization, industrialization, urbanization and weapons technology have produced sensitive people determined to claim it as an ally—therapist, counsellor, priest or elected delegate for civilization and its discontents. But the burdens have been loaded on to a phantom which has wilfully evaded its reponsibilities, preferring instead to pare its fingernails and study its own exquisite form.

Now it is conceivable that the very word 'art' is coming to the end of its life. Certainly, some of the cruder attempts to exhibit the specialness of art have foundered in the face of the sheer scale of the contemporary input into the individual imagination. Denis Donoghue pointed out in his 1982 Reith Lectures: 'People have to ignore so much, these days, of what they see and hear that the outrageous doings of an artist are easy to deal with.' Artists may not regret the passing of the obligation to outrage, but they will be less keen on the prospect of being ignored.

Yet perhaps this dislocation of the word is really an optimistic development. After all, the future, with an increasingly 'industrial' emphasis in official thinking on the arts, is hardly auspicious for the kind of art we have been given. So perhaps a new, more precise consideration of how government money is diffused, of the way in which certain illusions of adequacy left over

*Gerald Graff, 'The Myth of the Postmodernist Breakthrough', *Triquarterly*, 1973; reprinted in Bradbury, *The Novel Today*, p. 225.

from the 1960s are fading and crude political or precious anti-modern attitudes are beginning to appear vacuous, will all make space for art once again to separate itself from these associations. Such developments could foster a saner idea of art, less entrapped by the complications of its recent history and its appallingly bad press. They could offer freedom. Nothing characterizes the current arts industry as much as its persistent requirement that its books, plays or paintings should do or be something even before they are read or seen. Customers are lured into bookshops by promises that the latest voguishly serious novel will provide historical perspective or reveal the condition of society. They are seduced by the relevancy of theatre or the political urgency of films. Assiduously they trudge along, usually to be bored and always to be afraid of admitting it. The fearful combination of art and relevance is not one the socially adept would casually disparage. Music audiences are not subjected to the same ferocious demands and, as a result, probably have a better time of it. But all suffer from the need to throw familiar nets over art, to reduce its strangeness, subjugate its otherness.

Freedom in this context would mean the freedom to confront the works devoid of prior associations and assumptions—the freedom to accept that, whatever art actually is, it must first of all be definably other, strange and exhilarating. If the changes now in the air offer this possibility to the new, huge audiences for the arts, then they should be welcomed with open arms.

What follows is a highly partial and prejudiced survey of the various elements that make up the present climate and the way in which they all point to an imminent and widespread process of change. It is an individual view, but it is intended to touch on most of the key ideas which animate this somewhat fraught world. It is written in the belief that private, individual delight and a profound uselessness are fundamental to the nature of all art, yet also in the belief that creativity is obliged, for better or for worse, to cope with its antecedents. In this century that means dealing with modernism and its aftermath. It is a generalization, or possibly a series of generalizations, and all generalizations are kinds of lies. But a reluctance occasionally to abandon the particular has doomed the Culture Club to become a mass of opposing cliques whispering breathlessly to each other from sumptuously upholstered armchairs. The club room is filled with a stagnant fug, an atmosphere in which the wise man may take the view that it is worth risking a few speculative exhalations.

2

THE PAST

It was after the Angry Young Men but before the Swinging Sixties. F. R. Leavis, the Cambridge critic, was visiting Oxford to deliver a lecture. His host, a postgraduate student, had spent some time desperately trying to engage the great man in conversation by dropping the name of every significant modern writer he could think of. But clearly the mind that had created the Great Tradition of the English novel was in no mood to respond. He remained unmoved until his host arrived at last at the name of Kingsley Amis. 'That man is making a living by attacking everything we stand for,' Leavis cried. The lampoon of university life in *Lucky Jim* had wounded him. He always had the habit of over-reacting to those whom he perceived as enemies, especially when they were really his friends.

It was a response which revealed an illusory chasm in the midst of English cultural life in the 1950s. On one side seemed to stand the disillusioned, left-wing, anguished types who had got it into their heads that there was something wrong with the country. On the other side was the cultural establishment, which ranged from Leavis, jealously defending literature and the universities as the only repositories of values, to the welfare-working mandarins who wanted to bring art to the people via the 'revolutionary act' of government subsidy. The establishment thought that art could improve people by exposing them to the highest levels of perception and morality and could thereby sustain civilization. And the anguished types? Well, in fact, they really thought the same thing, as their later life stories revealed: Amis and John Osborne, to name but two, both moved inexorably to the opposite political pole and now defend the traditional values of the craftsmanlike, no-nonsense novel or play. That is why Amis was really on Leavis's side all along and the chasm was a mirage.

So it was a phoney war, but it was spectacular. The sullen divide of the 1950s became the riotous confrontations of the 1960s. In art, politics and education the same battle was fought. It was variously interpreted as being between anarchy and 'standards', between emotion and reason, between censorship and permissiveness or, as Leavis would undoubtedly have observed, between mass civilization and minority culture. But it was a civil war. The world had moved on. The civilized hierarchy and the dissidents were making wan moves in a game that had long been abandoned.

The game had, after all, been in progress for an awfully long time, and the suspicion that both participants had been indulging in little more than wood-shifting until their time ran out had begun to grow. The opening had been played in the eighteenth century, but it was not until the nineteenth that the strategy became clear:

> Culture looks beyond machinery, culture hates hatred; culture has one great passion, the passion for sweetness and light. It has one even greater!—the passion for making them *prevail*. It is not satisfied till we *all* come to a perfect man; it knows that the sweetness and light of the few must be imperfect until the raw and unkindled masses of humanity are touched with sweetness and light.*

Matthew Arnold's synthesis was the supreme expression

*Matthew Arnold, *Culture and Anarchy*, Cambridge, Cambridge University Press, 1981, p. 69.

of the tradition of thought which had been attempting to produce a coherent vision of society and culture during the century up to the publication of *Culture and Anarchy* in 1869. Art was to be for all because that was what art wanted. Furthermore, art was good, overwhelmingly good, and forever restless to communicate that goodness. Add to that heady concoction the redefining of the role of the state which had been progressing simultaneously— in Robert Southey's words, 'There can be no health, no soundness in the state till government shall regard the moral improvement of the people as its first great duty*' —and the game is clearly in full swing. In essence the traditions in which both Arnold and Southey were writing had sprung from the industrial revolution and the subsequent growth of the cities with all the attendant traumas of deracination and fragmentation. The loss of a comprehensible religious and rurally based society demanded new ordering principles. Romanticism sought those principles in the self, the last mysterious stronghold against the crude domination by man of increasingly unmysterious nature.

They were humanist traditions founded upon a kind of visionary panic at the spectacle of a world being mechanized, centralized, secularized and drained of values. Religion had faltered before the clear-eyed partnership between science and commerce. Arnold's culture was to be the new visionary vehicle, the bearer of man-made, as opposed to transcendent, moral improvement. It was still conceived in a religious context, but it sprang from forebodings about the failure of religion to transmit values and to unify society.

The new surrogate religion was to have a new priesthood whose function was too sensitive and required qualifications far too specific to be filled by the

*Robert Southey, *Sir Thomas More: or Colloquies on the Progress and Prospects of Society*, 2 vols., 1829, Vol. 2, Coll. XV, pp. 424–5.

representatives of any one class. Instead the clergy was
to spring naturally from all classes, a highly selective
meritocracy which would service, preserve and define
the new repository of values. Thus the culture–goodness
link was forged. Meanwhile the Southey tradition was
busily forging the government–goodness link.

To be brutal, little more needs to be said, for this is not
an intellectual history; it is the history of how an
intellectual tradition finally became action, and the
nuances tend to get lost in the process. Furthermore, the
tradition can hardly be said to have developed much
beyond Arnold. Subsequent thinking has merely focused
the attitude in response to the even more ferociously
fragmenting forces of the twentieth century. Arnold's
most obvious successor, Leavis, radicalized the vision to
the point where culture became a jealously guarded
property of the elect. It became the fountain of all human
wisdom, and there was only the one fountain. The
ignoble, defensive, paranoiac side implicit in Arnold's
position thus became dominant—ironically, just at the
moment when art in Europe and America had begun
systematically to abandon its role as guardian of moral
and social values. But in England all values still resided
in art, and if you wanted some, you could come in. At its
worst this became a defence of the role of the university;
at its best it arose from an honourably dim foreboding
that the great parties and parades of Western culture
were coming to an end.

'For many reasons standards are much more in need of
defence than they used to be,' wistfully wrote the critic
I. A. Richards,* failing to note that reason had been
denied by Marcel Duchamp when he exhibited his urinal
in a gallery and that 'standards' were being held
responsible for the First World War.

These traditions provide the climate for the post-war

*I. A. Richards, *Principles of Literary Criticism*, London, 1924, p. 36.

development of the arts in Britain. Periodically people may have gone out of their way specifically to reject them, but at no stage has a genuinely radical aesthetic or social view been sufficiently dominant to unseat them. In essence they claimed to establish a sort of extrapolation of the artistic sensation of the sensitive few into a system of communicable truths of inherent goodness and unarguable necessity. 'This,' wrote Peter Ackroyd, 'is the strange alchemy of humanism, in which aesthetic standards can be transformed into spiritual and social needs.* Once the alchemy had been performed and the passively defensive phase of Leavisism had passed, it became simply a question of how best to disseminate the good news.

But, to repeat, the tradition, although founded partly in fear at the prospect of the loss of faith, was born in a religious context. By the time the thoughts became action—seventy-five years after the appearance of *Culture and Anarchy*—the religion had long gone. In its place was a riot of good intentions; the amateur philanthropy and wishful thinking of the Victorians was to be replaced by national, state-bound ambition. Suddenly there was the welfare state, post-war reconstruction and John Maynard Keynes, the great economist, whose extraordinary talents were directed impulsively at the arts and their dissemination. Furthermore, there was an odd upsurge of fascination with the fabric of national identity to which even Tory, Christian T. S. Eliot succumbed when he attempted to define culture: 'It includes all the characteristic activities and interests of a people: Derby Day, Henley Regatta, Cowes, the twelfth of August, a cup final, the dog races ... boiled cabbage cut into sections, beetroot in vinegar, nineteenth-century Gothic churches and the

*Peter Ackroyd, *Notes for a New Culture*, London, Vision, 1976, p. 117.

music of Elgar.'* Published in 1948, Eliot's essay aimed at a definition of culture as the incarnation of a nation's religion. But the point was that the two were separate, and the arts were another separate entity within them. In place of Arnold's visionary unity there was a willed and more consciously worked out plurality. Eliot's religion still provided a cohesive force, but without it all that was left was a series of disembodied lists. The lists could be forged into a distinctive national identity or flavour, but that could hardly disguise their subjectivity.

Meanwhile, during the war, the Committee for the Encouragement of Music and the Arts (CEMA) had established the basis of government subsidy. It became the Arts Council, with Keynes as its first chairman, in 1945. It was part of a package which included the National Health Service, national insurance, nationalized industries and free orange juice—all of them practical, pragmatic, centralized ways to a better future. It is no coincidence that, to this day, the arts and the health service seem clasped in a bitter embrace when it comes to arguments about money. The Mosers, the Halls and the Braggs are fated to have their consciences interminably pricked by the kidney machine argument. Why, it goes, should we spend money on fripperies like opera or theatre when there are machines which are guaranteed to save people's lives and of which we do not have enough? As opera becomes more expensive and medical technology promises ever more spectacular benefits at ever greater cost, the need to come up with an answer seems daily more urgent.

Yet subsidized arts were created in the belief that their significance in some way matched that of the other welfare benefits. Sir Peter describes the process as a 'revolutionary act', but in reality it lacked that dimension of vision. The fire of Arnold and Southey had

*Eliot, *Notes towards the Definition of Culture*, p. 31.

been replaced by welfare paternalism: people were to be coaxed into doing what was good for them whether it was drinking their orange juice or dabbling in opera. The culture–goodness–government trinity was to survive and be strengthened even if the goodness element was only a shadow of its former self—a merely humanist ideal, bereft of spiritual context.

To return to Eliot's list and its straining towards cohesion and identity: the illusion today seems all too evident. The vision of a benign, hierarchical consensus has the air of sepia-tinted idyll before the roof fell in. The seeds of fragmentation had already germinated. This same remote, nostalgic sense enfolds the 1951 Festival of Britain. It too aspired to unity, but now half an hour spent scanning the programmes is half an hour spent in an alien world. The will to see ourselves as one nation was so powerful that it inspired the writer of the introductory message to describe the festival as 'The Autobiography of a Nation', 'displaying through every means by which Man expresses his nature how we have honoured our stewardship and used our talents'. Having lost her empire, Britain was to retain her international role by a process of illumination. A radiant national purpose would shine forth from these islands; we would be an example to the world. But then the writer added a strangely complex and ambiguous note, as if sensing the fictional side of the affair: 'And, as in any autobiography, the manner of the telling will be as revealing as the facts we set down.' And so it was to be. It is the style of the Festival that we remember, not its dreams masquerading as facts.

But it was not an artistic event. The arts played a subordinate and healthily acceptable role within the programmes. The Festival Hall, was, after all, the one permanent building on the South Bank site. Meanwhile, across town, opera and ballet would just sort of happen because that seemed appropriate to a national self-image founded upon an aspiring internationalism. Indeed, that aspiration produced one of the most lasting effects of the Festival—the embracing by the establishment of modernist architecture. The South Bank buildings were aggressively modern and stateless. They betrayed a yearning to escape from the merely local, with all its recent associations. Forty years after the invention of the future in architecture, Britain had officially decided it wanted some.

So the arts were on the national agenda, though only shakily pencilled in. They were, after all, still quite evidently the property of the elite, something we should have about the place but not as important as new types of tractors balanced on top of pillars or radio messages bounced off the moon. It was still a case of luring people into the sanctuary and whispering explanations in their ears as they stood there awestruck. But it was the start of the physical realization of the traditions—applied humanism, aesthetic standards becoming social needs.

The arts, however, are one thing, art quite another. Hopes that art would follow the Festival's lead were implicit in the status that the arts had been accorded. Opera and ballet appeared as self-consciously high-brow events and as representatives of a cultural heritage perceived as accepted achievement, steps on the perpetual upward spiral of liberal civilization. Indeed, it is probably truer to say they were not generally perceived at all within the context of the Festival. They were there as a reflex response of little or no organic significance to those not directly involved. Style and design were the only artistic areas that can be said to have been genuinely integrated into the spirit of the Festival. But, in so far as the other arts had been included, it was assumed that they were ready to participate in the urgent drive towards the future.

In fact, art went out of its way not to participate. With unerring perversity the first major, publicly understood aesthetic movement after the Festival was an assault on the standards, aesthetic and otherwise, towards which we had all been nudged. Melvyn Bragg summed it up:

> Kingsley Amis and Philip Larkin came along and said: 'Hold on, we think all this is crap, actually. When we listen to jazz or pop music, look at styles of clothes or television, it occurs to us that values are not just to do with George Eliot or Beethoven. They are suspect, of their time and ain't much fun. We think that fun is fertile.' So they began to attack the notion that art could only be considered as the high ground.

The benign but insular internationalism of the Festival was getting its come-uppance. The flip-side of internationalism is loss of nationalism, and as the aesthetic shrine was assaulted, so too was the national. The disillusioned sneer was invented. It began to be painful to be British, a sensation later intensified by Suez. Angry Young Manism involved the perception of the uncertainty underlying Eliot's assumptions and the Festival's optimism. The idea of a hierarchical consensus of illumination and culture began to look like an excuse for the loss of an empire. Bohemian dissidence is, of course, nothing new, but its particular impact and energy at this stage was critical to the shift of emphasis in the notion of 'the arts'.

The primary consequence was that the language changed. 'The arts' gradually edged towards signifying opera and ballet, traditionally presented. 'Art', in contrast, now firmly annexed as the province of the long-hairs, became something exciting, dangerous, committed. It assumed an air of cantankerous risk-taking. It is remarkable—indeed, depressing—how much of the history of this phase can be told in terms of censorship battles. At the Royal Court Theatre or on television frontiers were supposedly tested in the belief that they reflected nothing more than bourgeois squeamishness. A tradition of art constantly agitating people, provoking responses and striking attitudes was established. And established is the word. Nobody could seriously have been in any doubt that these battles would be won by the liberals, and thus, in the twinkling of an eye, the tradition was embraced by the whole of the arts as its adherents made their way to the top.

Not, it should be added, that there is anything wrong with winning censorship battles; it is simply that the battles seemed to be all there was. Years after the trial of *Lady Chatterley's Lover* the 'expert' witnesses called to defend the book as literature admitted that they did not really think it was very good. But at the time winning was what counted and easily worth a mild perjury. The note of dissent and outrage was the internal as well as the external dynamic. Post-war welfare art felt that its sole function was to fight fights, make points and shout the odds. Indeed, the very existence of the fastidiously arm's-length Arts Council effectively endorsed the whole package from the beginning. Operating at arm's length means that you respond to what the artists do rather than make suggestions or direct creativity, so it was cash on the nail for the social pugilists.

Nothing, of course, had changed. Substituting jazz for Beethoven or Jim Dixon for Edward Casaubon is of little more than journalistic significance. The most in-fluentially public art of the 1950s achieved at best a slight shift in content; the expressive plain remained undisturbed. Indeed, the superficiality of the commitment to change and the underlying resistance to formal innovation is again revealed by the subsequent positions of Amis and Osborne. A play of Osborne's could as well deserve the epithet 'well-made', with all its connotations of lucid exposition and transparency of surface, as anything by Rattigan; while *Lucky Jim* is a happily humanist document which toys comically with the notion of an indefinable self but then resolves the theme into one of mere social success.

The over-documented decade of the 1960s saw the fragmentary pretensions of these developments reach their apotheosis. The new orthodoxy—that our instit-utions had had their day—was adopted on the one hand for political ends and on the other for narcissistic ones. The development of the national identity theme in drama led inexorably to an increasingly left-wing posture, a stance which, in an infinite variety of potencies, became the acceptable one for the arts industry. Meanwhile the riotous diluted-Dada ten-dencies—for obvious reasons generally more promin-ent in the visual arts—led towards the self-regarding, Arts Lab-based, anything-goes avant-gardism which occupied the remaining, more hedonistically inclined students.

American developments of the time set this domestic revolution in context. Abstract Expressionist painting, critically defined as the first true schism between America and European culture, had accepted and grown through modernism. In drawing attention to the process of painting—as in Jackson Pollock's drips—it had abandoned any idea of content at all. The paintings, initially at least, had no 'meaning': they were events to be assimilated rather than codes to be deciphered. In a parallel development the New York school of poetry was creating a language devoid of conventional poetic intention. The language drifted in the world, isolated and opaque, unable to find any content which could justify the resurrection of the old trickery. The power and unquestionable originality of these developments were enough to propel them across the Atlantic, but they arrived in a container with a good deal of additional baggage—the Beat generation, rock 'n' roll, teenage rebellion and street wisdom. It was a heady mixture, a culturally imperialistic drive which swamped the more feeble British revolt.

What did survive, however, was the British capacity for compromise. As I have said, developments in British art had hardly breached the Queen's peace. They were adaptations of content rather than revolutions of form. The liberal, humanist tradition remained intact, unwilling or unable to be seduced by the transcendental and formalist tendencies of high American art but all too grateful for the anarchic hedonism of the lower. What was finally imported was more 'anything goes'. The consensus now was that jazz was art, so it was only a matter of time before pop would be art as well. Pollock's rewriting of the rules of painting came to mean only that anybody could be a painter.

This dilution soon emerged as a peculiarly British phenomenon. Genuinely new work was incorporated in the noisy public expansion of the arts, but it came too late, just as architecture came too late to the Festival of Britain and modernism has in some respects come too late to the current revival of the English novel. Marcel Duchamp's bottle rack meant infinitely more than the contained iconoclasm of the 1960s. Yet there remained a kind of knowingness about the sixties pose, as if the decade's obsessions needed to be ennobled by their proximity to the modernist intellectual tradition. The 1920s had reinvented the world in the name of the imagination; the 1960s reinvented the twenties in the name of marketing. Surfaces acquired imposed meanings, historical and ontological, as the term 'art' was applied to everything as a *quality* to be glimpsed by the chic and the hip in its most transient manifestations.

Meanwhile Jennie Lee and Lord Goodman were pursuing their 'benign illusions' and leading the Arts Council to higher ground, financially at least. The money was expanding under a theoretically sympathetic Labour Government, and efforts were being made to construct a balanced national network. In effect, the aim was a compromise between metropolitan 'centres of excellence' and regional devolution.

The Council also felt obliged to embrace the more radical outpourings. In 1968 it duly 'responded' with a new activities sub-committee, quaintly half-composed of 'young people'. Predictably, it became enmired in the implacable anarchy of the day and succeeded only in stumbling vaguely towards something called the 'Arts and Community Committee'. This was an equally sad state of affairs, and impatience finally showed through as well-meaning liberals made catty remarks about 'anti-culture' and the impossibility of incorporating it in 'culture'. The anarchists went their own way, so the mythology goes, to a mortgage and Cortina in Pinner.

But the anti-art versus art dualism was established and, with it, the standard Arts Council newspaper story: why are we putting public money into this rubbish? What is astonishing is not that the newspapers took such stories seriously but that the Arts Council did and still does. Never mind, no serious decisions had yet to be made; the money was still growing, and the Council, in spite of the fact that the creative initiative had been seized by the long-hairs, could at least pretend that it discerned an aesthetic hierarchy linking Arts Labs and street theatre with grand opera.

Art thus seemed very publicly alive and, when closely examined, appeared to have its soft, humanist heart in the right place. The newly affluent punters, better educated and ready to sample the higher luxuries, came like lambs to the slaughter. Television and its new drama helped to politicize them, while the Sunday newspapers were speaking increasingly of a world of bright young artists with the world enviably at their fingertips.

But the sheer weight of the new and undifferentiated product was overwhelming. Commercial and subsidized arts were operating at peak productivity. Furthermore, with the anarchic elision of values of the 1960s, it was no longer possible to say with any certainty what one should read, hear or see. There was just the sense that one ought to be doing something.

It was like stepping out into a blizzard. What was one to think? How was one to judge? Who was Kenneth Tynan? The answer to the last question was the answer to all three. Tynan thought the thoughts, evolved the judgements. He was the most flamboyant and obviously famous member of a new breed of critic/journalist required to mediate between the artists and the punters. He had a willing audience. The middle class knew perhaps that the arts temple had been desecrated by the regional accents of the 1950s, but Leavis's groundwork in establishing them as a very select club, with sole ownership of something money could not buy, had not been wasted. The arts had not lost their social cachet. They were an acceptable luxury, and as growth led to surplus that was the particular superfluity that the middle class wanted.

Of course, like everybody else, they wanted what they knew; like everybody else, they were post-war liberal humanists, afflicted by nagging doubts, certainly, but nothing that couldn't be talked through. Popular criticism delivered a translucent version of art. All this avant-gardism was reducible to neat little formulae: *this* is about the crisis of modern man or, more commonly, *that* is political. The latter made life doubly easy because you knew you could keep up with art by reading the rest of the newspaper as well.

No harm in that unless we appreciate the gulf between what was being disseminated and the truth. The newly art-hungry readers could not conceivably be ready to hear what had actually happened to the arts in the twentieth century: that modernism had dislocated the self, traditional aesthetics, the relationship between subject and object, and humanism; that the possibility of expression of any kind had begun to seem remote; that meaning had slipped through our fingers, just as the real world had done in particle physics; and that the Western arts, in their highest manifestations, were no longer prepared to plod down the same old road:

> *Beckett:* Yet I speak of an art turning away ... in disgust, weary of puny exploits, weary of pretending to be able, of being able, of doing a little better the same old thing, of going a little further along a dreary road.
> *Duthuit:* And preferring what?
> *Beckett:* The expression that there is nothing to express, nothing with which to express, nothing from which to express, no power to express, no desire to express, together with the obligation to express.*

This was not a symptom of self-indulgent, intellectual languor; it was a crisis as profound as any of the manifold crises of science to which we have paid so much attention. But its implications were unacceptable as any kind of product description. So what the public got was a highly confident, buoyant, celebratory expression of a communal loss of nerve. It was an anglicization of the problem, with all the characteristic English stubbornness in the belief that nothing had really changed. Compare Beckett's analysis with the view expressed by Martin Amis in a recent review of Kafka in

*Samuel Beckett, *Proust and Three Dialogues with Georges Duthuit*, London, Calder, 1976, p. 103.

the *Observer*: 'After the process of assimilation, however, we can see that only the art is innovatory and that the concerns belong to the mainstream of life in its humour and its pathos.' Nothing could be further from the truth, but certain industrial imperatives require Amis to be right.

But so distanced have we become from the 'hard idea' of the truth that Beckett's cold summary of the dilemma seems like a pose. Beckett himself was fine in the heart of the blizzard—he had been championed, after all, by Tynan and Harold Hobson—but the edge of his art was blunted by a spurious topicality. His work was said to portray some specific crisis of modern man. The trick was to shoe-horn the writer into the old category of expression—back on to the dreary road.

Still, what was lacking in seriousness was made up for in quantity. Expression positively littered the streets. With the advent of the Swinging London mythology the democratization of art attained its most effective incarnation. Tourism was being stimulated, and seemingly creativity had become marketable. After all, as we shall see, even dress was deep. This generalized sense of new energy provoked the suspicion, which the Festival of Britain had struggled so hard to create, that we were indeed a nation with exciting, innovative qualities. Perhaps a new post-imperial internationalism could be established after all. Even the Americans were now saying that we were the centre of a new kind of civilization, so perhaps a national identity could be forged on the basis of a democratized aesthetic. It was no accident that the Union Jack became a familiar and oddly ambiguous emblem of the 1960s. Anything, remember, could be art.

Then came the listings mag. This remains the only genuine innovation in the journalism of the period. It aimed to supply the ingredients of a good time for the fighting, cool and aggressive street wizards of the new radicalism. *Time Out* provided a wondrously cohesive view of the world, the importance of which, in this context, lay in its adoption of the arts as part of the wizard's essential armoury. And they were not going to be easy. A new high in critical opacity was achieved by the short reviews, particularly of films, that went with the listings. Underground movies were recommended in prose that defied analysis.

The layout of the magazine betrayed its intention both to explain and confuse. Sure enough, it organized the events, but at the same time it gave the profoundly depressing impression that there was so much to do that a life time was not long enough. And the critical voice was so consistently recondite that it seemed that there was just one person out there taking in all those shows. Years later the odd side-effects of this presentation came to light. A member of one of the most prominent rock bands of the period spoke about the way in which his gigs were listed as opposed to the cinemas, galleries and theatres. The band could always be relied upon to put on a good show, but next door there was a film dealing with some stupendous crisis of pre-revolutionary life. The band felt that this was a little unfair, so they were driven to more ambitious works, abandoning the simple song format and going instead for big-time expression. Art imitated journalism in fragmenting life in order to impose a political order.

One final symptom of the creative fever ought to be mentioned. It is a commonplace that sexual freedom had been closely identified with the liberationist ideals of the 1960s. Earlier censorship battles had created the link between supposedly the most pioneering art and permissiveness. In the 1960s a critical element in the new middle-class hankering for culture was the sexual one. The bright, creative young things had expropriated

sex. It was associated with freedom of expression, which
in turn partook of the fruits of the tree of art. The very
word 'free' was intended to denote imaginative freedom
on the one hand, yet on the other it retained the archaic,
derogatory overtones of promiscuity ('free with her
favours'). Typically, the moral and political force of the
insistence on imaginative freedom thus drew its real
energy from the oppressive past. Freedom would have
meant nothing for the few hundred who were swinging
in London had it not been for the stationary millions in
the rest of the country.

Furthermore, sex could not simply be sex. Inverted sex
became part of the process—indeed, a central part.
Homosexuality has long been associated with creativity,
with a sort of decorative and diverting uselessness, but
now it took on a fashionable tone.

In the 1960s it was all part of good living. Admittedly,
there was often a feeling of weariness and shabbiness
about the whole issue, but this was taken to be part of the
aesthetically endorsed sense that Britain was passing
through a phase of gracious and fascinating decline. The
neat decapitation of such indulgence by the oil crisis and
the generally dismal mood of the 1970s are now almost
as familiar as is the relentlessly documented iconography of the 1960s. In the theatre another phase of
unpatriotic anguish was embarked upon, this time with
a harder left-wing edge. Elsewhere, as it became clear
that the secret of perpetual economic growth had not, in
fact, been discovered, the mood changed from expansive
to defensive. But it was in everybody's interest to
pretend that nothing had happened, so that is what
everyone did. The Sunday newspapers remained much
the same, and the blizzard continued. But the audience
had changed: both its patience and its money had run
out. Evidently there was no brave new world round the
corner, so deep dress and Arts Labs were just grubby

phenomena characteristic of the old. Audience and industry, uncomprehending, began to drift apart. The people wanted cosy virtues, so television provided them with scores of costume dramas about a more stable and benevolently hierarchical past. But the avant-garde clung on, slumped once again in sullen opposition and assuming its traditional role of bourgeois-bashing.

After all, if there is one thing that the oil crisis and the subsequent testing of the banking and industrial systems of the West did for the artistic community, it was this: they endorsed the left's theme and its mythology and, consequently, its need to feel that art was important because it had big themes. For what bigger theme could there be than the collapse of capitalism?

3

THE NEW ARTS

'Style', wrote Angela Carter in *New Society*, 'means the presentation of the self as a three-dimensional art object to be wondered at.'* These words were, of course, written in the 1960s, when, as we know, anything could be art. In this case clothes were being shown to be deep. There is at work here some diluted structuralism, a recent French export. But the use of the word 'art' shows that the insight is still well within the terms of the old debate. What is it there for? To demonstrate seriousness, to validate the hedonist's aspirations to significance. But, in case that was not enough, the point is later rammed home:

> The Rolling Stones drugs case was an elegant confrontation of sartorial symbolism in generation warfare: the judge, in ritually potent robes and wig, invoking the doom of his age and class upon the beautiful children in frills and sunset colours, who dared to question the infallibility he represents as icon of the law and father figure.†

Now, of course, the judge and the Stones seem to have been in cahoots, providing material for the earnest Ms Carter. But then it was all new. Clothes had ceased to be the correct or incorrect uniform for particular occasions and had become externalizations of the self for the

*Angela Carter, 'Notes for a Theory of Sixties Style', *New Society*, 1967; reprinted in Paul Barker (ed.), *Arts and Society*, London and Glasgow, Fontana, 1977, p. 32ff.
†Ibid.

benefit both of the wearer and of the hip observer. They had become expressed self and, like the very idea of self, derived their energy from the degree to which they were different from others. And in this innocently narcissistic era self-expression in any form was art.

At this point the 1960s were clearly trying to have it both ways. On the one hand, there was the democratizing, anarchist impulse to call anything that involved self-expression 'art' without regard for discrimination; on the other, the decade wished to protect the magical value of the word 'art'. The publicity industry that supported the swingers did, after all, depend on the willingness of an aspiring middle class to continue to aspire. If mere anarchy were to be loosed upon the world, was it really necessary to buy the *Sunday Times*?

So, in the midst of this tightrope act, the new arts were created. Once the bourgeois-bating of the 1950s had cleared the ground, something positive had to move in. It arrived in the form of dress, lifestyle and, most significant of all, rock music and design.

Rock has been defined as a form largely by its impulse to seriousness. Its random roots have been elevated to the level of coherent tradition in the attempt to draw it into the mainstream of permissible art. Like dress, it invited the hip inside the select club of the newly aware. On the surface its elementary musical attractions made it accessible at once, but inside it provided strange mystifications, private languages of fantasy, eroticism and liberation.

That pop and rock, in spite of the claims made by the British to the form in the 1960s, were American-based is unimportant, as the national variations pale into insignificance before the international similarities. And besides, the enthusiasm and flare which the British brought to the form demonstrated a local need. But the requirement that it should be serious faced two problems: first, demonstrably it was not, in that it clearly pandered to the lowest common denominators of taste and experience; secondly, those instances in which it had been a serious reaction in the United States— black music, for example—could scarcely be recreated in Britain, a country sadly lacking in big issues with which to validate self-expression. The loss of an empire did not immediately suggest a guitar solo.

Both problems were solved by the mechanism of history. Once it had become clear that the Beatles were art, then, in the best English critical tradition, their antecedents had to be identified. These were duly discovered, and Elvis Presley was moved a few notches up the cultural ladder. But earlier manifestations clearly lacked the instantly recognizable, wider significance of the later material. 'Eleanor Rigby' had all the familiar dressings of alienation, but it would have been pushing the argument a little far to make the same claims for 'Jailhouse Rock'.

The next stage was to endorse the products as spontaneous reactions to their context. Indeed, the very unmediated crudeness of the reaction guaranteed its authenticity. The final product could be seen as relating directly to contemporary events. Art as recording angel, image and expression of the age became rock's primary aesthetic—if it occurred to you to put a pig in goggles on your album cover, then you had to do it because it was necessary to go with the flow.

The identification of this electric connection between history and performance became the function of the 'serious' rock critics. It was easiest and most potent when an Englishman was writing about a black American:

James Brown will die on stage one night, on the moving staircase of his own feet in front of a thirty-piece band; and then who knows what may be unloosed between black Americans and white? In Baltimore or Washington or Detroit, cities where the very peace between them has a quality of angry breathing, merely the presence of Brown has been reckoned to equal 100 policemen. Harlem, on the sweltering night after an atrocity, he can cool by one word. At the end of each performance he sings the chorus 'Soul Power' over and over again with bass guitar equalling a tribal tom-tom in rhythm that locks up the mind; but he doesn't cause a riot, he empties the theatre. The audience dances out into the street.

Oppressed people are the ones who need heroes in the deepest sense of idols that come from among them and can show them a way upwards to release and happiness.*

The real world of race riots and real death is required to authenticate the imaginary one of art. With what awe Norman notes the equation between Brown and a hundred policemen! This is effective art. Who needs the crisis of modernism when James Brown is sending them dancing out into the streets?

In Britain, of course, nothing seemed to matter quite that much, which was a problem. The liberationist tendencies required real oppression, and the American blacks had evidently cornered the market. So the impulse towards oppression became diluted. If we were not actually victimized by Mayor Daley and his policemen, there had to be something else. There was: alienation.

At least we were lost. A wistful tone entered the music as rock defined itself as the autobiography of a lost generation. The Who were aggressively British and also

*Philip Norman, 'James Brown: Mister Messiah', in *The Road Goes on Forever*, London, Elm Tree Books, 1982, p. 109.

aggressively lost. The comic litany which made its appearance in rock's later, mannerist phase, that of 'sex and drugs and rock 'n' roll', was intended to evoke not pure pleasure but fragmented automatism. The inability to get anything together was worn like the red badge of courage.

Thus in popular culture the dislocation of self had washed ashore as teenage sulkiness. The ephemeral, on-the-road, improvisatory qualities of mainstream rock provided the real dream of leaving home to drift. With that came a new pastoralism, a sentimental back-to-nature movement made grotesque by its love of electronically amplified music and the appalling devastation wrought by huge outdoor festivals. Then, as the lost generation lost its youth, the historical element became even more important. The more extravagant flights of myth-making in rock were increasingly a hypertrophied sense of lost childhood, symptomatic of a generation's reluctance to grow up once its own teenage fantasies had been endowed with such gorgeous significance by the Grateful Dead, the Who or the Band.

Perhaps this prelapsarian aesthetic could be ascribed to the innocence of the form itself. But was there really any form? Mostly it seemed like the juggling of fragments of minor musical traditions into a temporarily acceptable style. A meaning—generally one that opposed spontaneity to reason, or anarchic, romantic love to organization—was attached, and the product was lovingly launched.

But, just as the 1970s saw the growth of a mistrust of the avant-garde, so the decade produced a distancing from the extravagant claims made for popular music in the 1960s. As the angelic, existential layabouts became the new tax-exiled recruits to the old 'ex-pat' circuit, so the realization grew that they had just been another passing fad of popular music. Like the Angry Young

Men, they were revealed to be the true representatives of the very tradition that they appeared to have dismantled. Punk was a suitable enough response, but by then who was listening? Outraged by being ignored, the punk bands created a new meaning: they were the fruits of unemployment, and we were back on Beckett's treadmill of necessary expression.

Yet, inevitably, the sheer energy of the rock industry produced some genuine artists. Humanism crammed into three-chord sequences could hardly satisfy Bob Dylan, who evolved a cunningly meaningless form of song from the shreds of all too obvious meaning. 'I Want You' or the wilder tracks on his pirate albums seemed to arise precisely from the trance-like condition that had created popular music in the first place. Tim Buckley allowed an exquisitely lush musical form to crack under the burden of his own erotomania. Randy Newman loaded his deceptive structures with as much irony and indirection as they could bear, and Gram Parsons took the highly mannered form of country music and burdened it with an intense, emblematic selfhood that finally appeared to rear up and destroy him. And the Velvet Underground, Andy Warhol's most vivid creation, plunged into the truth of rock 'n' roll's Dionysiac hatred of self, expressed as sensory overload. It produced the most perfect rock track of all, 'Sister Ray', which had the effrontery to take the form at its true human face value—nil.

With these exceptions, however, rock music provided the kind of neatly packaged meaning that the new artiness required. Ponderous neo-critical standards were applied to increasingly dubious material. Art was handed to the people, not as a pre-existing corpus of attainment but as a *quality* that could be glued to anything. The notion retained enough difference and discrimination to preserve its aspirational value, but broadly its chief significance came to be its representative or symptomatic qualities. Art could be discovered anywhere, on the spur of the moment—particularly since pop music could be heard twenty-four hours a day on a transistor.

This impromptu aesthetic was also behind the new fascination with design. Like pop, it was everywhere, and, again like pop, it had the ability to take on conveniently topical and immediate associations. It also, helpfully, crossed the boundaries between the arts pages and the home and leisure pages: the lifestyle aspect of the aesthetic was always its most cherishable element for the middle class. A Braun mixer could be art or gadget.

Perversely, this fascination arose in a climate of surplus and superfluity, while the art of design itself was still firmly entrenched in the austere functionalism of the Bauhaus tradition. The Braun mixer was a case in point. Rayner Banham once described how he indicated to a conference in Germany that this mystical object might have design shortcomings. There was a deadly silence, followed by sporadic hissing.

Clearly, this messianic faith had to be diluted for the languid 1960s. Yet it could not be abandoned because modernism had defined 'good' design, with all the necessary moral context of the art that was longed for. There was no suitably weighty alternative. The result was a kind of expensively glitzy functionalism leavened by a cool wackiness, as exemplified on television by *The Avengers* or on film by *Barbarella*. Terence Conran made modernism widely available, with the added imperative of taste, in his Habitat shops. Irritatingly, this development coincided with a distinctly impure Victorianism that had arisen from the same roots as the increasing obsession with the past in other art forms. It turned out to be no problem. the Conran-Victorianist could live in a hundred-year-old house in which all the wood was stripped and the walls were painted white. This was not, after all, to be upholstered Victoriana, so it could claim some of the elemental simplicity of modernism.

Meanwhile back at the Braun mixer factory another contradiction between the aesthetic and the real world had surfaced. The aesthetic said that the form should be an expression of the function. Structure and mechanism should be expressed in a way that testified to a virtuous circle of truth. Unfortunately, with electrical gadgets this was impossible, for obvious safety reasons. The Bauhaus disciples kept their cool, however, and went for plastic boxes, undecorated and devoid of any bourgeois trickery.

The reason why all this has anything to do with art is not only because the enthusiastic critics in this field, as in so many others, wanted to convince themselves of the importance of what they were talking about but also because the design problem lies close to the heart of modernism. The notion of 'good design' encapsulated the moral thrust of modernist architecture, with its insistence on transforming the world and its utter lack of humility when confronted with the human scale. The revulsion against decoration was a revulsion against the trimmings of Romanticism and a yearning for absolutes in an unheroically secular world. That this scale of consideration should be engrossed in a food mixer or a toaster is an indication of the contrived and destructive nature of the aesthetic hierarchies that had been at work.

Now the argument has hardened even further with the emergence of a new decorative school variously called ornamentalist, post-modern or whatever. At one level this may be interpreted as the logical marketing move—to provide toasters with flowers on the side just to catch any sales you might otherwise miss. But in fact it was the same retreat that was reflected in one form or another in every other art (and of which I shall speak at greater length in chapter 6). Perhaps conscious that all this might be leaving the reasonably discerning punter behind, in 1983, Heal's, the London furniture store, held an exhibition entitled 'Whatever Happened to Good Design?'. The implication was that the public had been carefully educated in the idea of a moral absolute connected with the idea of design only to see a sudden riot of evidently frivolous colour explode on the scene.

Meanwhile, with an unusual degree of formal elegance for such a history, modernism was being driven into the galleries. Conran, clearly now a businessman rather than a cultural evangelist, set up the Conran Foundation and chose Stephen Bayley to run the 'Boilerhouse Project', a modern design gallery in the bowels of the Victoria and Albert Museum. Bayley is Conran's aesthetic conscience enjoying an out-of-body experience. He has remarked:

> It would be dishonest of me to deny the amount of influence Terence Conran has on me—I mean me personally. He constantly encourages me not to be afraid to say something. I perhaps say things Conran wouldn't say because they would alarm the City.

Bayley also confesses to being almost Stalinist in his belief in the possibility of absolute standards of design. He has little time for conservationists and a significant habit of idly polishing the stainless steel arm of his chair as he speaks, which neatly reflects the obsessive cleanliness of his vision:

> If I have a mission, it is to remove clutter from the

world. There is an imperative to remove clutter from
the world.

With this goes a love of tightness and discipline, the need
for rules of design which work beautifully with the food-
mixer aesthetic:

I like the idea of artists having to compete with each
other to attract the most mazuma. I'm not saying that
food mixers are as exalting as great works of art, but
there's no doubt that the processes that went into them
are similar to the processes that went into a work of
art.

These people really have a tight brief to fulfil. They
actually are required to go out and lead the public. You
have to understand what motivates people and leads
them a little further than they would have expected.
Surely this has something to do with art....

The attitude also does away—healthily—with the
aesthete's usual squeamishness about commerce.

If you buy a Sony TV, it does add a measurable amount
of quality to your environment. It is a little bit
exalting; it adds genuine pleasure. A Braun calculator
enhances my desk. Architects always have Sony
televisions—I've never seen an architect with any of
the other Japanese brands.

The basis of the Bayley–Conran aesthetic is, in
essence, that design is where the greatest visually
creative energy is now concentrated. Its view is
democratizing in the same sense that the great
modernist architects were democrats—that is, in
a visionary, messianic sense. It is now regarded
with suspicion (and indeed some hilarity) because
of its aspiration to absolutes in a world that has
sunk back into a relativist mire. In Bayley's hands

the aim of the aesthetic is to unseat the academy and the market:

> The only people who are interested in painting these days are extremely wealthy people who are told to buy something.... I'm fascinated, and indeed delighted, to see the prices of Impressionist paintings begin to tumble.... It's a sham and charade largely inhabited by charlatans and poseurs.

Jim Dixon in *Lucky Jim* always used to laugh at arty-farties and their strenuous poses and pretences. But really for him the arty-farties were the modernists with their foreign aesthetics and Continental habits. Bayley also laughs at them because they have abandoned the truth—ironically, in view of his own love of commercial products, because the workings of the art market have got the better of them.

Everybody now agrees that design is an art, but just as the consensus was arrived at the problem became hopelessly complicated. The art that everybody had agreed upon was late modernism (slick plastic boxes, plain colours and hi-tech functionalism), but suddenly another seemed to be gaining ground—riotous colours, superfluous detail and trashy graphics.

> At this particular moment [says Bayley] there really is a crisis in values. Nobody actually knows how to judge. There is a nostalgic longing for an order that was lost in the eighteenth century, when the mass market was established and taste exploded over all the population. You can see the modern movement as a means of imposing standards.

The new arts have arisen, in the case of rock, from an upgrading of what people did anyway and, in the case of design, from a sudden need to endow taste, as expressed in functional artefacts, with greater significance. Both movements demonstrate the way in which the terri-tory of art is prone to invasion not simply from good work outside its traditional sectors but also from generalizations arising out of a need to believe, a need to be taken seriously, a need to get on the membership list.

4

THE MONEY

Henry Wrong strolls round the Barbican Centre, an ambiguous smile on his face. As far as the punters are concerned, the administrator is smiling, so all is well; employees are more likely to detect the pained fixedness of his expression, a certain tightness around the jaw line. Wrong holds his dinosaur of an arts centre together with facial muscle tone.

He eats with some distaste in the restaurant when he has no choice and makes lightning security checks in the small hours of the morning, descending from his Barbican *pied-à-terre* with fastidious wrath. He makes his entry into the vast set, with its chandelier, an object expressive of nothing so much as the cost of light fittings these days, its bush-hammered concrete sporadically concealed by large orange sheets of plywood and its baffling 'levels' as opposed to floors or storeys. The light is low and the carpets thick. You might be in the foyer of an American bank.

It is a fitting monument for the Canadian Mr Wrong to wander through in the small hours—a monument to all the dogged uncertainties that have characterized Britain's post-war public funding of the arts. It is perhaps embarrassing that it has clearly been built to last five hundred years—presumably to become one day a symbolic relic to be deciphered by amused historians.

They will find it a rich source of information about our age, for at the Barbican the art–money equation has achieved a weird kind of formal perfection. To begin with, it is in the City, the money-making centre of the nation. If one locality might reasonably have been expected to be free from the lure of post-war welfarism, this was it. But first the City decided it needed people living there; then it decided they needed some kind of recreational facility; and finally it found, to its amazement, that it needed a £200 million international arts centre.

It was an exquisite piece of non-planning, which occurred solely because of the local government anomaly that retains the medieval identity of the City and gives it a rateable value of breathtaking size. As a result, of course, the nation finds itself with an enormous sum of money to spend on the arts but discovers that it can be spent only within a particular square mile of London in which there is absolutely no tradition of artistic activity.

The organic growth of London has decreed that entertainment should be in the West End and commerce in the East, but the organism reckoned without the sudden onset of a mania within the City Corporation to make themselves a real, rounded city. The one thing they do inordinately well is to make money, so perhaps it was merely a subconscious longing for balance which drove them to the arts, which can always lose it with such style.

This bumbled evolution is reflected in the day-to-day relationship between the authority and the centre. There is a governing body, which is a committee of the corporation and therefore not the sort of governing body Britain's largest arts centre might expect to have. Its inexperience leads it to dwell at a somewhat bemused distance from the centre and, specifically, from Wrong.

Wrong is a pragmatist who builds and runs arts centres. Wider qualms are not his stock in trade. He is our only representative of that latter-day breed of global, cultivated autocrats who run the prestige subsidized centres around the world. He is managing to keep afloat a centre which is appallingly expensive to run and which houses the Royal Shakespeare Company and the London Symphony Orchestra. Relations with the former have been reasonable but for its tendency to lapse into a habitual arrogance, and with the latter terrible owing to its distinctly unpredictable management style.

The theatre seems to be all right, having at least been given an auditorium comparable with that of the National. The record of the art gallery has been un-impressive, and the concert hall has created a massive over-capacity in the serious music business in London.

But the real point is that not one of these amenities is necessary. They arose from a liberal itch to do something: in the event, to build an arts centre in the wrong place. When the imbalance between what London possesses without the Barbican and what provincial cities possess in total, the scale of the madness becomes apparent.

Perhaps the centre's real problem is that it is obviously a symbol. It took so long to build (nineteen years) that by the time it was finished its architectural style had not so much gone out of fashion as become an object of derision and moral outrage. It reeked so obviously of 1960s urban planning that the whole tidal wave of indignation at modern developments that have obliged old ladies to climb thirty flights of stairs when the lifts break down was unleashed upon it. It is the real monument to the Festival of Britain spirit.

It is also a monument to the way in which money invested in the arts in Britain tends to end up in the wrong place and in the wrong form—as capital rather than revenue. This is particularly tragic in view of the fact that the arts in this country are enjoying a period of unprecedented wealth. For a start, they now occupy prestigious new buildings like the Barbican, the physical realizations of the liberal impulse. Less obviously, they can also lay claim to vast and constantly marketed capital resources resulting from the value added to paintings and sculptures by the operations of the expanded international art market. They are just beginning to tap the revenue available from the rapidly growing world television industry. They can logically expect to benefit to some extent from the generally increased leisure time available to the population as a result of technological advances. Orchestras are supported by recording and film work. Opera and theatre are beginning to exploit video as well as broadcast television. Painters are supported with energy and determination by galleries possessed of a seemingly endless and irresponsibly eager list of customers. Novelists are suddenly back in business with the emergence of a large promotional thrust for the 'serious' novel. Radio and television provide outlets for writers on a hitherto unknown scale. Private corporations are steadily beginning to discern some merit in artistic patronage.

Sure enough, all of these things are ambiguous delights. Recording in London is in decline. Video exploitation is producing only tiny sums for the national companies. The art market is unpredictable (note the swift decline in impressionist values) and has been as much damaged by recession as any other industry. No growth, and probably contraction, can be expected in Arts Council funds. Television is highly specific in its demands. Commercial sponsorship is capricious and irregular. But the fact remains that the scale of the arts industry is large, and when electronic dissemination is taken into account, there has never been such a huge potential audience. It is in this context that the constant grumbles of the arts world should be seen. Their complaint is the malaise of affluence, not poverty.

But money and art have never coexisted easily.

Evidently there are two sources of cash, the market and patronage, yet neither produces simple solutions. In the case of the market Raymond Williams has identified in *Culture and Society* the acute pressure which immediately arose when an affluent middle class became interested in culture during the industrial revolution. It began to buy literature and to aspire, a process spectacularly accelerated, as we have seen, two hundred years later. But 'the free play of genius found it increasingly difficult to consort with the free play of the market,' writes Williams.* In other words, the obligation to sell seemed to taint the obligation to express. Patronage, on the other hand, appears to take it as read that art has an intrinsic and unquestionable value and it is made available to cushion the artist against the full impact of the free market. Unfortunately, patronage imposes its own restrictions: there are only certain types of sculpture that can be placed in churches or which IBM will tolerate. When it comes to government patronage the problems become mind-bogglingly complex and produce ever more fraught extrusions of logic and clammy moral distinctions. Money and the arts now live in a variety of uneasy partnerships, neither really acknowledging the scale of the uncertainties underlying their relationship. At each point of contact the pressures at work are extraordinary, but the grumblings of the one side and the doubts of the other should not blind us to the central fact that there is an awful lot of cash around.

The trouble with affluence, of course, is that it creates perpetually rising expectations; if a poet in residence, why not a painter? If an arts centre, why not fifty? And so on. The democratization of the concept of art, although aimed primarily at creating wider audiences, has had the dubious effect of creating more artists. As the sphere

*Raymond Williams, *Culture and Society*, Harmondsworth, Penguin, 1968, p. 63.

of those participating directly in the arts has expanded, so more people have aspired to join them. Rapid growth and wider publicity in the 1960s, as well as the apparent arbitrariness of much of the work, led to the feeling that money of one type or another was the right of any reasonably creative activity. Note the ambiguity of this sentence from Lord Goodman's statement in the 1969 Arts Council annual report: 'Within our society there is now a widespread feeling that the provision of drama and music and painting and all culture in its broadest sense is no longer to be regarded as a privilege for a few, but is the democratic right of the entire community.' The 'few' or the 'entire community' could be providers or recipients of art. The question was left dangerously open, and the Arts Council to this day has not decided whether it is looking after audiences or artists. Similarly, in the wholly commercial sector fashionable patronage of new writers or movements by publishers, galleries or broadcasters has oscillated between the two, stimulating and frustrating expectations in quick succession.

Yet the industry in which these oscillations and ambiguities occur has sustained explosive growth over the past forty years. This growth has both produced and been confronted by a variety of recent problems. Most obviously it has run into the malign combination of recession and a government whose primary policy decision will restrict growth in public spending for the foreseeable future. Lord Goodman's 'widespread feeling' that a right to public cash existed clearly does not extend to all the ranks of the modern Tory Party.

The clash between the old liberal conviction that government should fund the arts more or less unquestioningly and a right-wing market-economy party has provided a steady stream of fairly basic publicity. Every week or two one arts organization or another is claimed to be on the brink of oblivion. The

anti-Tory sentiment behind these stories and in the arts
world as a whole has suddenly found them a remarkably
flexible and useful means of expression. For one thing,
the arts retain their image as worthy and hardworking,
in contrast to other publicly subsidized industries. For
regular audiences they also have a warm, clubby air
which provides a very different emotional environment
from that of those other recipients of taxpayer's
resources—undecorated hospitals, recalcitrant dustmen
and cantankerous car workers. It was the perception of
this peculiarly ambiguous political role of the arts which
prompted the Greater London Council and its far-left
leadership to turn the arts in London into one of the most
visible issues in the fight to save the GLC in the face of
Tory plans to abolish it. Ken Livingstone and Tony
Banks could see more mileage in the Royal Festival Hall
than in any number of black lesbian collectives.

In the event this is a superficial reading, based more
on what people say than on what they do. On the surface
Mrs Thatcher's Government has pursued a rigorous
macho-monetarist line. The arts, in this climate, must
take their chances along with the National Health
Service. At first Norman St John-Stevas as Arts
Minister attempted to get round this problem by arguing
that the policy of rolling back the frontiers of the state
could have 'no logical application to the arts'. Perhaps it
was a brave and sane stance in the circumstances, but it
mystified the less transcendentally logical members of
his party, who simply asked: 'Why not?' His present
successor, Lord Gowrie, began by attempting to combine
an unquestioning belief in the Government's economic
policy in all areas of life, in the universe and in
everything with a brief to defend the arts. He resol-
ved the contradiction by speaking evangelically of
improving management and efficiency among the Arts
Council's clients, a phenomenally weak posture, which

left him speechless when cuts had to come.

Yet perhaps everybody should have listened more closely to the Minister. He did not mean simply that we would all have to tighten our belts as best we could—or if he did mean simply that, his words are about to be radically reinterpreted. What has happened is that the arts have suddenly vaulted into the larger economic arena. Without broadcasting and publishing the industry is thought to have a turnover of about £1,000 million. Taking in broadcasting and publishing, the figure rises to about £2,000 million and, adding in ancillary economic effects, to as high as £3,000 million or £4,000 million.

These figures are guesses: nothing else is available. There is a prodigious level of statistical ignorance in the arts industry. Nevertheless, the sums involved are quite obviously large and, as all the arts are notoriously labour-intensive, they must also represent an army of arts employees.

Of course, the arts lobby has always been vociferous in its attempt to convince the world that it is not just a pack of aesthete ninnies. With the advent of Thatcherism the clamour swelled. Indeed, social and moral benefits were seldom spoken of; instead the key arguments became economic. In a memorable television programme transmitted on the BBC on 20 December 1980 entitled *Arts UK—OK?* (a title whose only claim to decency was the question mark) Joan Bakewell summarized this case in jauntily optimistic style, considering with arch self-deprecation the wonderful and spiritual world of art as profitable business. 'They actually make a profit for this country,' she explained happily. The problem with this attitude is that it betrays a kind of snobbery. All right, runs the argument, we all know how great the arts actually are, but slumming it a little for the benefit of the accountants, let's show how efficient they are too. The relationship that is implied is hardly an organic, exemplary one.

Perhaps conscious that the economic case was looking a little tenuous and even slightly offensive when expressed in these terms, the Arts Council decided to go for a more subtle analysis. They wheeled in Professor J. K. Galbraith to deliver the W. E. Williams Memorial Lecture at the National Theatre on 18 January 1983. Galbraith's lecture was limited in scope, but he did go for the soft underbelly of Thatcherism:

> One of the miracles of modern industrial achievement has been Italy.... Italy has been an economic success over the last thirty-five years because its products look better—because Italian design is better. And Italian design, in turn, reflects the superb commitment of Italy to artistic excellence extending over the centuries and continuing down to the present day.*

This improves on the Bakewell posture because it adds to the mix the non-financial quality of national success. Note the mingling of seemingly transcendent values and purely practical ones. Compared with the merely economic defence tailored for the Tory voter (as in Bakewell's case) or for the Labour voter (as in the case of Melvyn Bragg, who is convinced that Arts Council 'seed' money in urban areas has a useful job-creation function), the Galbraith line is the winner. It offers both the carrot of the market and the vision of national glory—the Falklands spirit plus mazuma.

But the case is still being put by the wrong side. Galbraith may add weight to the arguments, but his support also appears childishly provocative in the present climate—he is, after all, the economist most absolutely opposed to the Thatcher ideology.

*J. K. Galbraith, *Economics and the Arts*, London, Arts Council of Great Britain, 1983.

However, in October 1982 the House of Commons Select Committee report *Public and Private Funding of the Arts* was published. First the report endorsed the central position of the arts in national life and acknowledged that they did not seem to have enough money—so far great news for the Arts Council. It then went on to recommend significant decentralization of power and substantial organizational changes which would, if fully implemented, massively reduce the workload of the inhabitants of 105 Piccadilly. The report has proved increasingly influential: it was self-evidently thorough and it made many points that the Government had not even considered. The context of the debate had been changed.

Then came Clive Priestley's scrutiny of the affairs of the Royal Opera House and the Royal Shakespeare Company. This was ordered by the Prime Minister as the price to be paid for the additional £5 million one-off payment to the arts made in 1983–4. In the event Priestley was almost embarrassingly nice to both companies. Criticisms were minor, comments no more scathing than scrutiny of any organization would be bound to provoke. Overwhelmingly the conclusion was that both needed more money. In addition Priestley suggested direct funding from the government, bypassing the Arts Council. The Select Committee had only gone as far as suggesting earmarked funds to be channelled through the Council.

Meanwhile Government plans to dispose of the top-tier local authorities—such as the GLC—were coming to fruition. Demonstrating clearly the way in which the arts had moved up the agenda, the fate of the arts organizations funded by these authorities was almost the first issue that arose from the Government's plans. The official response was to make a list of arts organizations deemed to be of national importance, which would receive central government aid. The rest could sink or swim on whatever other money they could find. Oddly, although this scheme seemed to move in the same general direction as the other two documents— away from the Arts Council—it opposed them in one key respect. It would result in less rather than more localization of funding. But these were early days, and the crude point was the important one— Whitehall muscle was being applied in the field of arts subsidy.

The implications are clear enough. In waking up to the size and significance of the arts industry, the Government had also become alert to the fact that its prime means of intervention and involvement in that industry was via a somewhat eccentric organization, which seemed to involve itself in highly publicized rows with appalling regularity. Priestley's report had inquired politely why Arts Council officers needed to be present at every board meeting at Covent Garden, while the Select Committee had wondered wistfully if the 8.2 per cent administration charge imposed by the Arts Council once the national company grants had been disregarded was not just a little too high.

These were deadly asides. Ironically, just as the Arts Council was winning its battle to convince the Government that it was a major and profitable industry, sections of the Government were forming the view that the industry was too major for the Arts Council.

The potential for change arising from this Government's awakening is enormous. The old Goodman defence of the Arts Council is based in its role as an extra-governmental body which neutralizes the cash, strips it of any possible political clothing. This precious arm's-length principle is fiercely defended as the organizational soul of the council, which justifies its existence as the launderer of money and preserves us from nasty Continental excesses of the Ministry of Culture variety.

History, however, can be rewritten. Perhaps the arm's-length principle was born not of an idealistic urge to protect the freedom of the arts but of the continuing squeamishness in Government circles over subsidies for the performing arts. In 1945 such subsidy still had a slightly improper feel to it. Thus the portion of the Arts Council's defence that is based on its traditions is being questioned.

In most other areas its defence looks similarly weak, primarily because of its disjointed history. Also in 1945 Keynes, with uncharacteristic lack of foresight, suggested that public money need concern itself only with the bricks and mortar of the arts; audiences and artists would look after the rest. In other words, provide the capital and the revenue will roll in. In effect, his advice was followed. Especially when Jennie Lee was Arts Minister, the Arts Council made investments the precise revenue consequences of which were not foreseen.

It was a miscalculation, based on a belief in the efficiencies of scale, that now has a familiar ring. Small was ugly in the Wilson years. Tiny, scattered units had to bear separate sets of overheads and were thus intrinsically less efficient than big, centralized ones. Furthermore, those were days of hope and belief in what technology could achieve, so the attractions of drafty church halls and rooms above pubs were not yet evident to even the most hardened Bohemians. So, for example, it was seen as desirable, and even potentially cheaper, to move energetic local repertory companies from their shabby, improvised premises to purpose-built modern theatres next to local Tescos (and looking very much the same).

Simultaneously the major national companies were being established and knitted into the fabric of government funding. The policy was to proceed logically and smoothly, in best Wilsonian order, towards a combination of international metropolitan centres as flagships for a process of diffusion throughout the regions and a system of regional centres ready to be diffused to.

In fact, the goals set were unattainable at the levels of funding then current and completely out of the question once growth had stopped. The legacy of those unrealistic aims is an ill-structured subsidized sector with little semblance of regional commitment. There is a wild imbalance in favour of London and a grotesquely assorted ragbag of fringe and ultra-fringe companies on the Arts Council's client list.

This does not exactly leave the Council in a position of strength from which to defend its traditions from the inroads of the Priestleys and Select Committees of this world. Its traditions and inclinations are overwhelmingly in favour of preserving its policy of 'response' rather than leadership informed by an ideology of welfare idealism. This policy (or non-policy, as many have said) has been executed over the years primarily by Tony Field, the Council's amiable finance director, who has either run the place single-handedly or failed to throw his weight around enough, according to different observers. His opinion now is that there should be a radical and, where necessary, ruthless decision to go for the old 'centres of excellence' strategy. Resources would be concentrated in big regional centres, and the client list would be pruned ferociously. This approach is based on the perfectly sane accountant's view that waiting for a bunch of out-of-work actors to form themselves into a company, with all its ancillary bureaucratic obligations, and then funding it in the traditional 'response' manner is absurd in the present climate. Existing small companies should be pushed into existing studio facilities in the purpose-built theatres, and so on.

Field's general—though not so far specific—strategy won sudden and unexpected support in November 1983, when the Ilkley Letter was dispatched to all the Council's annual clients. This plan had been conceived at a major meeting of the Council in Ilkley, and the letter asked all the clients to reply, very quickly, to two questions: first, how would you respond to a large (say, 25 per cent) increase in your subsidy? And, second, how would you respond to a large (say, 25 per cent) cut in your subsidy? In a brilliantly revealing passage Luke Rittner, the Arts Council's secretary-general, gave the rationale:

> The arts, like seeds, need to grow if they are to blossom. Some of the seeds we have nurtured over the years are now bursting to grow but are held back by lack of space and nourishment. This strategy will help the Council to thin out the seed-bed to give more room for them to develop, and for new seeds to be planted.

So, just as Field had recommended, the Council was seen to be taking hold of its own destiny. It was accepting that the days of growth had gone and was planning for the real world. In the context of the three government documents the letter can be regarded in one of two ways: either it is a general defence intended to show that there is still life at 105, or it is the brainchild of Sir William Rees-Mogg and Luke Rittner aimed at taking up the challenge implied by the new Government thinking.

Neither possibility makes perfect sense, and the strategy may be ill-conceived. But, taking the latter as the more likely, then it will, presumably, come up against the kind of resistance from which Field has always suffered. This arises from the ideology of the infantry at 105 Piccadilly, which is broadly soft left and has a protective attitude towards the Council as it has evolved. Both Field's position and the Ilkley Letter imply a move towards a substantially more clearly defined posture. Whereas the soft left will always have perceived some link between the vague, unspoken non-policy of 'response' and the vague, unspoken qualities of art as dreamed of in their aesthetic, Field and the Letter suggest a wholly new relationship. Gone would be the mistily organic link, and in its place would be determined statements, choices, decisions. A hierarchy would be imposed. The Council would stick its neck out. It would no longer claim to have its finger in every possible creative pie; it would simply say that it believed it had chosen the few really good plums. People would be free to disagree. Such a muscular response would threaten to sever the weak thread of the romantic inheritance which still runs through 105 Piccadilly.

In fact, Field himself embodies the whole contrast between the sentimental and the muscular poles at the Arts Council. He has long advocated this tougher policy. He is, after all, an accountant who yearns to have standards by which he can run his affairs. Clarity is what his plan would offer and so, ultimately, might the fallout from the Ilkley Letter. But he has always suffered from a particular weakness in putting the case, and it is this that now might put him out of sympathy with those whom he has suddenly found on his side. The weakness is his own devotion to the psychological and emotional traditions of the Council, a sentiment which appears even stronger than his impatience with the financial ones. Field is fascinated by, and grateful for, the quality of the debates he has witnessed during his twenty-six years at the Council. He remembers certain moments with fondness—like the occasion when Lord Goodman warned him of the folly of providing Joan Littlewood with more money when she was in the midst of producing shows like *Oh What a Lovely War!* and *A Taste of Honey* at Stratford East. 'Be very careful with your arguments,' his chairman warned him. The point was that money could wreck creativity as well as nourish it. It is a paradox which exists in the liberal mind as an enduring rebuke to the accountant's view of the world. Field's confidence in that view is perhaps not therefore what it might be, and his long and respectful apprenticeship at the Council may prevent him from leading it into the new post-Priestley dawn.

So the Arts Council's will to live is being tested. The Ilkley Letter is its attempt to respond to the chaos of its inheritance. One aspect of this chaos I have mentioned already—the confusion of intentions and the trauma of the end of growth. There is another, more specific area which should perhaps also be mentioned. This lies at the other end of the painful money–creativity nexus, and in a sense it is the most obvious problem: how much money do you give people? The idea behind subsidy is that it frees desirable creativity from total dependence on its ability to compete in the marketplace. Subsidy may be needed to encourage innovation or to safeguard expensive arts which are seen as socially beneficial but cannot pay their way unaided, or it may simply keep ticket prices down, making culture more widely available. The logical conclusion of the subsidy ideology would be to give tickets away free and to pay for everything out of the public purse. The argument against this is that it would sever any organic connection between artists and the audience.

From this problem arises the idea of a balance of subsidy, a correct level which both frees the artist and obliges him to attract some kind of audience. The balance may be different for different organizations, but at least prior to Priestley it could be taken that the 60 per cent of revenue from subsidy towards which the Royal Opera House was heading, and which the English

National Opera had passed, was too high and the 12 per cent at which the London orchestras operate was too low.

This theory has a comical and genuinely revealing impact on one's perceptions. There are the London orchestras, with their faintly anarchic reputations, their bitter in-fighting, gossipy managers, unruly brass sections and wheeler-dealing pursuit of the fast buck, whether it comes from knocking off Beethoven's Fifth at the Barbican or plugging cigarettes at the Festival Hall. The point is, of course, that their low level of subsidy makes the orchestras competitive in a somewhat undignified way. This is aggravated by the fact that there are four London orchestras putting on hundreds of concerts and all competing for the same relatively small audience. In the present climate they have very little creative latitude, and in any case there is a constant tension within the orchestras between the desire to go for maximum earnings for individual members and the inclination to go for the highest possible standards.

In reality, of course, there are too many of them and too many concerts. Unfortunately, Arts Council subsidy is filtered through the London Orchestral Concerts Board, which adds to it the Greater London Council's subsidy and then doles it out roughly equitably. This means that there is no mechanism for taking difficult decisions. If any orchestra is going to die, it will have to dwindle slowly over a period of years. Furthermore, restructuring is made doubly difficult by the heavily unionized nature of the industry. In short, the orchestras are unpleasantly strapped to market forces, and all that subsidy does is to distance the usual bottom line of the market—bankruptcy. Management convulsions and constant rumours of simmering revolt are all traceable to this basic tension.

At the other end of the subsidy balance an eerie calm prevails. The two national opera companies, the Royal

Opera House and the English National Opera, certainly worry but not with the same leaky transparency. ENO takes some 70 per cent of its revenue from subsidy and the ROH around 55 per cent. No organizations could be further removed from the squabbles of the orchestras. Here the minds are forever on higher things, perennially in pursuit of some exquisite high—or at least the best operatic anecdote about the good old days or (as the past is well known to be another country) about the magnificently well-endowed opera houses abroad.

The problem has been the catastrophic level of exposure. When the ROH and the ENO between them absorb 17 per cent of an Arts Council budget of about £93 million, it is clear that they are obliged to be at the sharp end of the subsidy argument. They stand as the gross examples of conspicuous consumption which the hundreds of impoverished Arts Council clients dutifully lambast. Priestley's wisdom may lie in his realization that only by separating such grandiose arts entirely from the rest of the field can opera truly be protected from such unpleasantness.

Of course, rows over relative levels of funding have always incorporated all the other big grievances of British life—class, the regions versus London, left versus right and so on. These have an unnerving habit of escalating at once into conflicts on the broadest scale, not least because of the heavily political emphasis placed on art by so many Council clients. And it is in this context that the other half of government policy, the encouragement of commercial sponsorship, also runs into trouble. There are all sorts of practical reasons why the arts have resisted the approaches of companies anxious to promote their names in the right environment—the unpredictable nature of the cash flow and the need to discuss programmes being the obvious two. In addition there is the capitalist taint that sponsorship has been felt to cast over all it touches and, of course, there is a touchy distaste, deeply entrenched in the English consciousness, of money arising from mere trade.

Yet commercial sponsorship is the nearest that this Government can get to 'privatization' of the arts that will certainly never pay their way in a real free market. The example of the United States is usually proffered when the arts moan that there is just not enough money, but there is a key psychological difference between conditions in the two countries. For a start, money for the arts in the USA does not come primarily from companies; it comes from individuals and not necessarily spectacularly wealthy ones. This generosity is prompted in part by the unqualified odour of sanctity that emanates from the arts. They retain their unambiguously upmarket appeal. But there are also tax incentives, and it is now clear that some similar system has been under serious consideration here. Unfortunately, the Treasury has resisted the removal of VAT from theatre tickets long enough to make it obvious that official thinking is not moved by the plight of the arts to the point of fiscal concessions.

Without such concessions corporate money has been trickling in, a process accelerated somewhat by the encouraging climate created by the Government. But the relationship remains edgy. Few people seem to have learned to live with the true psychology of commercial sponsorship. On the one hand, it is an arm of marketing aimed at showing the company flag as prominently as possible and at associating its name with something self-evidently good; on the other, it is a sort of glorified lunch, a particularly lush brand of entertainment, suitably exquisite and refined. In this latter category Glyndebourne is the obvious example, surviving to produce high-quality opera without the aid of a single public penny. In his 1983 programme George Christie, the general manager, even rallied his private-enterprise troops by bragging of their independence of central government funds. This was a delicious example of doublethink: look what private enterprise can do, he was saying, appealing to a political stance which places its reliance on the market. But Glyndebourne is as much protected from market forces as the National Theatre. It is insulated by large-corporation vanity, not by its rugged competitive ability. Nothing wrong with that, of course, but let's not confuse the issue.

Yet, ideologically acceptable as tax incentives for private sponsorship would be, that does not look like Lord Gowrie's most probable route. To gauge his likely course of action it is necessary to combine the impact of Priestley and the Select Committee report. As I have said, the report identified the nature of the industry. Priestley demonstrated that the message had been received. Previously whenever civil servants had been confronted with the arts they had displayed a proud ignorance. Usually they would suggest that opera companies should cut the size of their choruses to save money. When it was pointed out that the remainder would be drowned by the orchestra, they smirked and had the last word: 'Ah ha, not if you cut the size of the orchestra.'

But Priestley is different. He does not simply defend the cost of opera; he defends it in detail. At first this may appear to weaken his case: he mentions the top layer of an underskirt for a Covent Garden Donna Anna in *Don Giovanni* which cost £140, but he then justified the cost by saying it had to last a long time.

This type of perception, plus the Select Committee's rigour, will probably push the Government towards a high level of devolution to the Regional Arts Associations, and the Arts Council may be slimmed down and left to deal with strategy and the broad level of allocation. This may actually produce more money for the arts, as experience in other countries has shown that in the right circumstances greater local involvement has produced greater willingness to subsidize. It would also work to offset the anomalous regional structure which the Arts Council's disjointed history has created.

Finally, there is the real market where people have to make money to survive. In essence, the problem for art here is the same as the problem in the subsidized sector: how to protect minority culture against the requirements of mass civilization. In the case of the recording industry classical music has been living reasonably healthily with its 8 per cent share of the total record market, though its profitability cannot compare with that of the pop business. In addition, recording costs in London have been driving the companies overseas, while the impact of home taping has threatened the delicate balance which protects the record companies' capacity to offer the choice. The same sort of balance is required in publishing, where 'serious' work rides precariously on the back of an industry of immense variety which nevertheless sees itself as obliged to retain its role as an artistic patron.

But in the real capitalist world developments have occurred which will inexorably transform the market for the subsidized and the profitable alike: briefly, these developments involve raising the cash from the pockets of the true potential audience. Sir Peter Hall points out that if he puts on an opera at Glyndebourne, within six months it may well have been seen or heard by several million people, thanks to radio and television. 'It has to be hand-made and excellent in the beginning to be broadened out in that way,' he says, adding, 'and what's elitist about that?' The point is that although opera on television may draw a tiny audience in relation to

Coronation Street, it draws a massive audience by comparison with any theatrical production. The problem is making the punters pay.

At the moment a television or video company simply puts up the money and shoots the production or, increasingly, puts up the money for the original director to shoot the production. This is fine but not massively profitable, and it leaves the original subsidizer with most of the production bill. The balance of power should switch slightly with the advent of cable and satellite television, as the broadcasting companies will require huge amounts of new material simply to fill their schedules. At the moment the arts companies are picking up mere scraps from this source.

Yet the new techology's true impact will not be simply upon cash flow; it will also strike at audiences. If satellites can bring live musical performances to people's homes from any part of Europe, then the attraction of staying at home may be too much for even the most hardened concert-goer, and in any case the subscription cost is likely to be substantially lower than buying the equivalent number of tickets. Thus the paradox arises: television will need something 'hand-made and excellent' to broadcast, but it may threaten the real viability of that hand-made excellence by taking away its live audience.

The final point is this: the arts are unprecedentedly wealthy and, assuming they can learn to live with the problems, should become even more so as a result of the new technology and increased leisure. But the problems of applying money to art as such will always remain— first because quality is a minority interest and, second, because nobody is ever sure what is the best. The consequence is continuous friction, a constant failure of the money and the art ever quite to understand each other. Their mutual incomprehension is exacerbated by the tendency of post-war Britain to throw the same social, political and moral nets over cash as it does over art. In any age the artists tend to make their way somehow in the direction of the cash, though these days they may feel obliged to agonize over its moral connotations first.

Mozart died in poverty, and many more Mozarts will go the same way. 'How rich he would be if he were alive today!' exclaimed Sir Peter Hall. Fair enough, but how poor Blake....

5

SOME MANDARINS

On the whole they are gossipy, agnostic, complacent. Some have developed the techniques of man management—the narrowing of the eyes, the drawing out of the interviewee, the refusal of the pay rise; others are content to rest on the laurels of their calling, preferring an amiable openness to go with their priest-like function. These are the mandarins to whom we give money and from whom we expect art in return. 'This priesthood had to be created,' explained Richard Somerset Ward, head of BBC Music and Arts, 'in order to be respectable among the artists on the one hand but also to be acceptable to whoever was giving out the money. We've created a rather odd type of person in this country. I'm one myself, actually.'

Odd they certainly are and of unpredictable pedigree. In fact, in this respect they precisely fulfil Matthew Arnold's dream of an elect drawn from all classes to administer the sacred mysteries of culture. First, there are the reformed radicals who sprang from the creative optimism and organized iconoclasm of the 1960s. As the 1970s progressed, they gracefully shifted gear, later to become the chairmen and board members of the 1980s. It was a transformation effected by many people in many walks of life, and, as we have seen, it was not as startling as it is sometimes portrayed. But its stylistic effects remain, most obviously in the ex-radicals' longish hair, their patronage of the young and the note of nostalgia they often find so hard to suppress.

Second, there are the existing establishment figures.

Successful in other walks of life, they join the ranks of the great and the good and are able to pursue a love of the arts as enthusiastic amateurs.

Third, there are those who, intoxicated by the arts at an early age, discovered they could not be directly involved but succeeded in taking advantage of the explosion of administrative posts that occurred during the period of post-war expansion.

Almost to a man the mandarins are soft-left egalitarians at heart—again Matthew Arnold would approve. 'Men of culture are the true apostles of equality,' he wrote.* Occasional lapses like the odd well-publicized vote for Mrs Thatcher should not be taken too seriously. Their views are generally predictable, usually self-justifying, though nowadays with an added note of ironic self-deprecation, as if the welfare arguments for the arts have become faintly embarrassing, to be wheeled out only when the question is asked. Perhaps this is because they sound merely local at a time when they have all found themselves operating within an increasingly international market for their services. Arts administrators tend nowadays to be as much in demand as producers and directors. This has forced them to broaden their horizons, even if only contractually, perversely enough just at a time when new art has become deliberately more parochial.

But, easy as it is to generalize about these people, it is necessary to listen carefully even when they do not seem to want to talk. Geniuses may come and go, but the managerial side of the arts business is, at least in theory, controllable. These intermediaries between public and artists have awesome power. They define the words for us. When we think of the arts in general we are more likely to have Messrs Hall, Bragg and Strong in mind than any specific work or artist. Their roles vary from

*Arnold, *Culture and Anarchy*, p. 70.

the purely administrative or financial to those on the
borderline of administration and creation, but they are
to be considered as a whole because they all share the
same power. Presumably they are the future as well as
the present, as a new generation of entrepreneurial
visionaries does not seem to have arisen. Their
accommodation with the abyss above which they are
obliged to work gives us some inkling of what to expect.

But first an oddity—Henry Wrong, whom we have
met before. Only he is genuinely a product of the
new international market in arts administration. A
Canadian, he runs our only all-round international-
scale arts centre, the Barbican, and as such he stands
outside the British system, a representative of a less
tortured, less doubting breed for whom most of the
questions have long been answered.

Yet mainstream liberals will have no trouble with
Wrong except perhaps on the matter of style. His
sentiments are well within the accepted parameters of
opinion on the subject of the arts and how to raise money
for them. Perhaps he errs too far on the side of the overtly
populist, but then he has to feed his dinosaur of a centre.
Stylistically, however, he is more pragmatic than the
rest. Being Canadian, he lacks the ability to hide his
function behind a façade of sociability and idealism.
When giving quotes on the record he can scarcely
suppress his laughter at their discontinuity with what
he would say off the record. He asks advice, and gives it
in return, with a dash of flattery. For choice he lunches
at Wilton's and drinks at the Savoy American Bar. He
has a talent for conspiratorial speculation. Half an hour
spent with a relaxed Wrong can be hair-raising.

It is less fun if you lunch with him at the Barbican.
There are constant interruptions as he hollers at the
waiters to clean fingermarks off the stainless steel or
assails you with a critique of the quality of the food. He is

given to pained and prolonged speculation about the
structural and political background of his pet dinosaur,
speculation which tends unexpectedly to take in everybody with any influence, up to and including the Prime
Minister. He is a practitioner who seldom asks why but
often how. For Wrong the war has been won. He is there
to keep the show on the road by mopping up (when
necessary) the odd hostile straggler.

Perhaps we do not have enough Wrongs. After all, as
Sir Claus Moser has said, the question of whether
central government should fund the arts is simply not
asked abroad, a phenomenon which gives foreigners a
certain disturbing confidence. Only in post-imperial
Britain do we torture ourselves. Wrong gets on with the
job. Yet, useful as his position is, it is not one that casts
light on our central quest for the ideas that animate this
little world. Before leaving him, however, one last
attribute should be noted: he has no taste, a fact that he
readily acknowledges.

He is not alone. Mandarins as a breed find it difficult to
come to conclusions on artistic matters. They bounce in
and out, enjoying them or not but seldom really judging.
In fact, of course, such an incapacity is an invaluable
asset for mandarins who have to move among the arts
with tact and strategic enthusiasm. For them the arts
have to function daily. If they work, then questions of
value need not arise. Partly this is because there is
simply no need—critical discrimination would get in the
way of the higher pragmatism. But also it is because the
boundaries of discernment soon get blurred by the lure of
friendship, good turns, favours owed. It is best not
to possess too exclusive a vision in this world. The
significance of this, of course, is that art need not exist.
All that is required is the notion of 'the arts' as a separate
and qualitatively superior activity indulged in by the
members of the club, for whom the unwritten rule is that

you must be in rather than out, not good rather than bad.

A more useful figure in the ideological context is Melvyn Bragg, a highly active club member who conveniently operates within the subsidized structure and also presents the arts for our delectation on television. His are perhaps the most instantly recognizable name and face when the subject of the arts is mentioned. His *South Bank Show* has wrong-footed the BBC by providing glossy and convincing coverage of the arts without obviously degrading them.

The show itself takes much pleasure in variety. Its title sequence celebrates the multiplicity of the arts and, tellingly, their inter-relationships. It is an animation showing Beethoven metamorphosing into the Beatles, pens and pianos, not to mention the Sistine Chapel ceiling, brought to life with real lightning. These liquid elisions are evidence enough of the liberal optimism at work behind the conception; the message is that Beethoven and the Beatles are one—something does join them, something probably secular but still mysterious. As Leavis might have said, if you want some, come in.

Appropriately, Bragg's career—his move from novelist to television at the BBC and then finally to *The South Bank Show*—is a paradigm of the 1960s success story. Throughout he has been a loud and confident defender of the arts and of subsidy. He sees himself as an old-fashioned Labour voter ('There aren't many of us left') and defends arts subsidy as a great example of socialism in action. Now he works in a corner of LWT's south-bank tower. His wall is decorated with a huge 'projects in hand' board, which looks like something between a war memorial to the medium's battle to encompass the unruly arts—'Greene, Beckett, Márquez, Borges' and so on—and a moose-head relic of some high-brow hunting expedition. He is perennially affable, liked by all and touchingly willing to be argued against.

His belief in what has been achieved and in the need to preserve it is absolute. Public subsidy is the essential substitute for the decline of private patronage: 'Economic change has made that game impossible to play. Individuals don't have all that money. BP does, but BP doesn't know how to build an opera house. It's never going to.' So his socialism in the arts is based not on any bitter aversion to capitalist lucre but on the simple fact that it is not available to do this particular job. It may seem a sensible enough approach, but it does have its visionary side. He has a not very apocalyptic view of society in a state of collapse, with central monoliths crumbling and authorities being fundamentally and fatally questioned. In such circumstances for some people 'art can be the sustaining image of their lives.' But only for some people. Central to Bragg's analysis is the acceptance of the limitations implicit in an aggressively evangelical stance, and immediately he hurries to acknowledge that there are many other sustaining images: 'My father lives for sport,' he admits.

It is, in effect, the last line of defence of the welfare art view. It says that the high ground of Leavis and Arnold can no longer be held. But there is still a small hill with a sign on it saying 'Art', a sign which guards many against potential psychological damage wrought by the devastation and fragmentation around them, so the hill must be held. It is just one among many but, after all, the Sports Council still gets more money than the Arts Council.

His attitude to art is thus relativist in a relativist world: 'Anybody who's had the kind of education I've had will say watching *Macbeth* is different from watching *Coronation Street*. I would say at the same time that it's entirely possible that people get values from *Coronation Street*—they get enormous things from it which mean a

lot to them.' But he describes the saving grace of his
relativism as his preparedness to make large statements
about what the arts can mean to him. And this is where
he calls a halt to the retreat from the high ground. It is a
sane and logical place to stop, but it is still bang in the
middle of the motorway. Art offers the individual values;
values reside in art. For Bragg artists deliver the goods,
and he believes that the people whom he profiles on *The
South Bank Show* are the most important in the world.
But he is not simply attempting to convert others—
indeed such an attempt would no longer be acceptable.
Collapsed monoliths leave a lot of fragments, and Bragg
is simply claiming his right to say that he has found one
of the best.

And yet there is an even further retreat implicit in this
position because although Bragg makes vast claims for
the arts on his own behalf, his relativism prevents him
even from making the same claims for others who share
his view of their importance. This is the defence to the
usual jibe that Hitler liked Wagner and Mozart was
played in the concentration camps.

I know people who are doused in art, people at the
opera house every night. They are lethargic, lazy-
minded. This is where the attempt to describe art
through what it gives you breaks down. Because there
are other people who have nothing to do with art who
are full of life. I mean, I talk about illumination—but
there are people who've got that and they never read a
word. The guy that conducts the Black Dyke Mills
Band versus George Solti. I mean, it's a damned close-
run thing in many ways.

But Bragg will not—possibly cannot—make the final
retreat into the dissociation of art from values. A certain
puritanism, a residue of his nonconformist background,
demands that his pleasures should have some moral

basis, an educational foundation. He provides an extraordinarily vivid picture of a man constructing a shrine of his own among the ruins of the debate. He does so with a rare sincerity and frankness, but his way forward is more of the same. Characteristically for one whose quandary is so evidently at the heart of the matter, he is now engaging with the very latest development of the argument—the economic one. But Bragg is not one to make claims for the tourist-stimulating value of the arts, rather for their power to generate employment. He speaks enthusiastically of the effects on employment—as yet small but growing—of relatively modest sums of Arts Council 'seed' money in city centres.

Bragg's importance arises perhaps from his literary background. The consciousness of these matters stems from the English literary tradition in which the debate took place. His knowledge obliges him to spot the difficulties in any given position before he is unwise enough to adopt it. Sir Claus Moser, chairman of the Royal Opera House, by contrast, is endowed with a greater degree of naivety. Possibly he is closer to Wrong—he too is a foreigner (German-born), and his primary role is in the most costly of the arts, just as Wrong's is in the big-money, political climate of the Barbican. When it comes to opera Bragg, without admitting it, has a very English suspicion of the form. He makes points about the difficulties that Covent Garden has in defending its subsidy as a means of paying the going rate for international opera singers. But Sir Claus is proud of his involvement in the arts, and he makes the simplest possible claims for them all:

I see Covent Garden as important not because we employ a thousand people or because it's a place where people have glamorous evenings. I think that a great

performance of opera is something that makes people
attending it better people. I think one comes away
enriched and therefore in some sense a better citizen
and a happier person.

This view meshes effortlessly with policy: 'I think the
more people who get a sniff of great opera, a great ballet
or a great book, the more civilized a nation becomes.'

This, in essence, is Goodmanism Mark One, the view
of Lord Goodman in his heyday as chairman of the
Arts Council. Lord Goodman himself has substantially
modified the view. Now it amounts to a simple dissemination of material he likes and which therefore
other people should have the opportunity to like. The
visionary gleam which Moser still possesses has
vanished from the Goodman eye, to be replaced by the
satisfaction offered by a good lawyer's case.

Sir Claus himself is now a merchant banker, having
once been chief statistician to the Government. He
works in Rothschild's, in an office and at an address
which appears to have been constructed entirely so that
it could be described as at the heart of the city. He has a
broad sentimental streak, which surfaces most clearly
when he appears bruised by the very idea that anybody
should question why opera is a good thing. 'But the
reason I can cope with these constant attacks is the belief
that, when we get it right, 2,250 people do leave the
opera house slightly happier than when they came in.'
His sentimentalism leads him to contrast the worlds
of money and music as if constantly facing some
shortcoming in his professional career.

Sir Claus shares with Lord Goodman the conviction
that the argument can stand up at the simplest level. He
is impatient with any attempt to introduce metaphysics,
believing firmly that you simply have to look at the facts
to be won over. Failure to be won over he dismisses

as philistinism. Lord Goodman is shrewder in his knowledge of the enemy and sees that the real reason for avoiding complications is that they play into the hands of the barbarians raging at the gates, to whom subtlety is a sign of weakness. But Lord Goodman's shrewdness in weighing up the opposition makes his stance appear less sound than the sentimental idealism of Sir Claus. For one thing there is his insistence on reducing the debate to the level of pleasure, which constantly emerges in the form of food imagery:

> You don't have to be converted to Catholicism to enjoy good food. An impulse to eat some delicacy need not be a religious impulse.... I, Lord Goodman, have discovered that eating an apple is a very enjoyable experience. It then becomes a duty, a moral duty to communicate this enjoyment to as many people as have got teeth to eat an apple.

The problem with this is that it leaves only prejudice to differentiate art from other human activities. And at that point in the argument it becomes clear that there is no answer to Jeremy Bentham:

> Prejudice apart, the game of push-pin is of equal value with the arts and science of music and poetry. If the game of push-pin furnish more pleasure, it is more valuable than either. Everybody can play at push-pin: poetry and music are relished only by a few.*

But Lord Goodman is not alone in this constant resort to art as sensual pleasure and in the somewhat alarming reduction of that pleasure to one of the crudest of the senses. It betrays, on the one hand, a desire to make the argument open to as many people as possible by

*The Works of Jeremy Bentham, ed. John Bowring, Edinburgh, William Tait, 1843, Vol. 2, p. 253.

referring to the most commonplace of activities and, on the other, a mildly depraved conception of art. It is one thing to derive morals from aesthetics but to derive them from the experience of satisfied appetite would suggest an entirely new brand of liberal humanist hedonism. Such sensuousness cannot compete with Sir Claus's idealism, however wistful. Lord Goodman has given too much of the welfare ground away. Compare his words in a speech to the House of Lords in 1967:

> I believe that young people lack values, lack certainties, lack guidance, that they need something to turn to, and need it more desperately than they have needed it at any time in our history—certainly any time which I can recollect. I do not say that the arts will furnish a total solution, but I believe that the arts will furnish some solution. I believe that once young people are captured for the arts, they are redeemed from many of the dangers which confront them at the moment....

Sir Claus is still really of the class of '67 and is perpetually saddened rather than embittered by the battles he finds he has to fight. Before leaving him, mention should be made of a new battle in which he has discovered himself to be a combatant. This is a duel with the critics, who have grown wary of the sumptuousness of international-style opera.

> There are in Britain—and it's happening all over the world—music critics, a very particular crowd, who are more happy seeing a poor performance of an opera they've never heard of than hearing the best possible of *Trovatori* in the world. Hence there was the ludicrous picture last year when Harrison Birtwistle's *Punch and Judy* was put on at the Drill Hall and a leading critic said that this was what opera was all about.

Sir Claus liked *Punch and Judy* himself but is dismayed
by the cantankerous way in which its qualities are
praised above those of Covent Garden's standard lavish
repertoire. 'These people are perverse,' he says. In the
next chapter I shall look at the question of whether Sir
Claus is missing the point.

The gulf between Bragg and Sir Claus is perhaps
simply the gulf between the literary and the performing
arts. Sir Claus, with his remnants of liberal idealism, is
ill-equipped to cope with the storm, but at least he is
confronting it. Bragg, however, has a clearer knowledge
of the construction of umbrellas. Bridging the literary
and performance arts is Sir Peter Hall at the National
Theatre. He also conveniently straddles the commercial
and subsidized worlds, thanks to his involvement with
the electronic exploitation of his productions as well as
fully commercial shows.

Conveniently also, Sir Peter's career neatly encom-
passes the move from art as dissent to established
art. He ran the Royal Shakespeare Company and
imposed upon it a strongly political and polemical
flavour. Mistakenly, it is said that he imposed his
personality on all its work. In fact, his down-the-line
liberal/radical anti-censorship posture could not have
been more impersonal. What he did was to pursue an
active policy for art as a position in some great social
debate which was presumed to be taking place. Then, on
moving to the National, his method changed. Gone was
the cohesive company speaking with a single left-wing
voice. Instead a more passive managerial stance
appeared. A multiplicity of voices was to be encour-
aged as a correlative of the shouted debate taking place
in the world outside. Each play at the National is still
approved by Sir Peter, but the directors have to select
them first.

His image has always been problematic, more so since

the publication of his diaries last year. He has a reputation for scoring own goals, and his unfailingly relaxed air puts people on their guard, as does the hand that flutters perpetually before the beard, occasionally plucking. He appears to collect enemies at the same rate as friends, the latter claiming he is the only man to do the job and pointing to his directorial triumphs, the former claiming that the role of manager has swallowed him whole. 'There seems to be no inner life,' commented one recent reader of the diaries. 'That's because there isn't one!' snapped Jonathan Miller. What is clear is that Sir Peter is conscious of himself in the public world to an unusual degree. Being a major figure of his age seems important to him. His decisions are endowed with historical justification.

I ran a theatre in the 1960s in a way which was extremely polemical, extremely prejudiced and very much my view—the RSC. I came here and decided I wasn't going to do that at all and I've been criticized ever since. I decided it was my job to reflect contradiction, and chaos, and variety, and the spectrum of what drama should be at this particular moment, rather than saying the Olivier Theatre should be all Shakespeare, all Chekhov and so on. So I constantly try to be variegated.

The idea of art as a debate, an argument, takes its energy from the same social view as Bragg's—the concept of the fragmented monolith. However, unlike Bragg, Sir Peter holds the view with equanimity; counter-arguments are enclosed rather than confronted. Such is the determination of this approach that it leads him to the belief that, in fact, fragmentation is the most fertile possible environment for the theatre. 'I see society as something noisy, incoherent, full of argument, confrontation and contradiction. I think it is infinitely

complex and just as noisy as a good debate in the House
of Commons. We should all scream at each other.'

Thus at the drinks laid on for the press after the trial,
on obscenity charges, of National director Michael
Bogdanov over the play *The Romans in Britain*, Sir
Peter was in his element. Groomed and sleek, he
presided, having won another of those interminable
battles for freedom against the forces of oppression. It is
better to be a screamer *and* a winner. But, just as in the
1950s, the dice were loaded. The play had its message
neatly packaged with its glib format: the Romans
were just like the British in Northern Ireland. Even
if Mary Whitehouse had won, the left would have
smiled and remarked in knowing unison, 'Exactly our
point.'

But Sir Peter's relatively passive role at the National
is extended, in that he sees himself, when it comes to
staging new plays, as simply putting on the best that is
available. 'Show me the great right-wing plays' is his
answer to those who have criticized him for presenting
left-wing propaganda. Yet clearly, since he has a right of
veto over every play at the National, his idea of great or
good is fundamental to the meaning of his role. In
defining this he betrays none of the usual defensiveness.
He perceives theatre as a humanist art with moral
intentions. He did, after all, study under Leavis at
Cambridge.

If you ask somebody to spend two or three hours of
their life—which will never be given back to them
again—seeing or hearing something, certainly I hope
they will experience delight, but I hope their mind will
be challenged, they will question a little bit how they
live and what they do. It's a difficult position to define
because it sounds high-minded.

Added to this is his important use of the word 'hand-made' to describe the products of opera and theatre. Both, he points out, are labour-intensive industries which flourished, before the twentieth century, on cheap labour. But both have lost their chance of commercial viability in a mass-production age. There are two important elements in this use of the word 'hand-made'. One is the anti-industrial revolution slant it implies, and thus its relationship with the whole tradition of romantic thought concerning the function of the arts. The other is its sentimental post-1960s aspect. Along with this go Sir Peter's pleasure in the fact that people sit on the carpet in the National's foyer and his distaste for modern architecture. In addition there was his response to Tony Banks, the somewhat riotous though astute director of arts and recreations for the Greater London Council, who wanted the National to go out to community centres around London. 'But what about *this* community centre?' responded Sir Peter, gesturing at the concrete and the carpet beneath his feet. That remark happily encapsulated the way in which the hippy socialism of the 1960s has been transformed into a faith in institutions, in the fabric which all that energy created.

In a sense there is no problem for Sir Peter. His Glyndebourne productions are televised, reaching ever wider audiences. He can put on a relatively unknown drama at the Cottesloe, and he will get an audience—indeed, 'The audience seems to be voracious.' Britain appears to have abandoned the worst excesses of its traditional philistinism, and culture is now OK. Sir Peter is the least ruffled by any suggestion of change; he skirts the question by interpreting his role as merely to mirror change and fragmentation.

This is the spectrum of the old guard. From Bragg to Hall they defend, with varying degrees of conviction, the arts as repositories and disseminators of values to a people which is becoming increasingly grateful. Except for Wrong they betray at one time or another an awareness that they are still being questioned about what on earth *fundamentally* they are there for. Fundamentals bother them all, with the possible exception of Sir Peter.

The depths and shallows of this agnostic, liberal consensus can be found throughout the arts. For most it is the only conceivable way of viewing the matter—any other approach is fascism or philistinism. And in the context of an aggressively right-wing Government any other approach can be explained as a conspiracy to intervene, to stamp out the old freedoms. Sir Claus Moser is now a card-carrying member of the SDP, a bureaucratic endorsement of the soft-left ideology which has nurtured the growth of the arts and which today finds itself allied with more extreme politics in the fight to keep the money coming.

In this light the appointments of Sir William Rees-Mogg as chairman of the Arts Council and, subsequently, of Luke Rittner as secretary-general could only be interpreted as the placing of the Thatcherists in the driving seats. In fact, this is a grossly naive view. Sir William, for all his monetarist sympathies, broadly believes in state subsidy for the arts and, indeed, that it should represent a higher proportion of government spending than it does at present. Rittner could not be more pro-arts, though his work at the Association for Business Sponsorship of the Arts inspired fears that he was being brought in simply as a lure for private rather than public money.

Rittner was also regarded as a calculated insult. The liberal consciences at 105 Piccadilly had trouble with this one, but in essence they were hurt that he had no O-levels. At the height of this crisis one senior officer, sweating slightly and in an extremely nervous condition, confided that basically Rittner was just not quite 'their type'. The liberal sensibility can take all kinds of deficiencies in social graces, but lack of education is all but inexcusable. 'It's an insult to us all,' he said. 'It shows just how we are being degraded.' He will have had his view confirmed by the Priestley scrutiny and was even then speaking with the memory of the anti-105 sentiments in the Select Committee report.

The somewhat cruel onslaught on Rittner has left a considerable scar. He mentions repeatedly that he is 'no intellectual'. He is affable, organized in his speech if not in his thought and one of those people who, having failed to enter the arts on the creative side ('Ever since I could crawl I wanted to go on the stage'), found that the post-war growth in the industry offered him another chance.

Rittner is one of those over whom the arts have exercised a hypnotic fascination and who has never seriously considered the possibility of spending his life in any other field. On starting his job he was subjected to a training schedule by Sir William, which meant that he was hardly in his office, a development that helped to confirm the crude view that Rittner was no more than Sir William's creature. Indeed, it seems to lie behind some of Rittner's remarks. '[Sir William] is clearly an intellectual. I am in no way an intellectual. He is probably someone who finds it more difficult to deal with people. I'm never happier than when I'm dealing with people.' Such a management-based rationale is unwise in the circumstances, enraging those who see Rees-Mogg and Rittner as a two-man rightist hit squad. Nevertheless, the rationale can be seen to spring from a desire to make the two men look different, and in fact Rittner's independence appears increasingly to be emerging.

Rittner is also a Roman Catholic, though somewhat shy on the matter. When dealing with Sir William religion is a good starting point. In his devotional book *An Humbler Heaven* he writes that he lives in 'a world which has lost its faith, which is like a fish out of water or a drowning man, desperately thrashing around for lack of oxygen'.* These are not the sentiments of a Candide-style liberal such as those who marched the arts from the Festival of Britain to today. They are the remarks of a deeply religious man whose vision is fundamentally opposed to the benign sociological optimism of the soft left. So although the old guard may be lulled by Sir William's evident commitment to gaining more money for the arts, it ought perhaps to be clear that it is dealing with a radically different animal.

It may, of course, be of no immediate practical significance. Managing an unchanging or decreasing sum of money most of the time gives little scope for Catholic right-wing or agnostic left-wing intervention. Day to day Sir William will protest, cajole, soothe or enrage in much the same way as previous chairmen of the Arts Council have done. But it is as well to remember that he does so in the context of a very severe system of priorities:

> I think that the arts are a part—but only a part—of the total development of man. It seems to me that we still have, in theory at any rate, the Renaissance idea of man as a fully developed person using all his capacities, one of those capacities being artistic appreciation. I don't myself see art as being as important as religion. I think it can contribute to a religious sense in that the highest art can exercise a relationship with a Platonic ideal which has a religious aspect to it.... at its most important art is a way of apprehending God.

*William Rees-Mogg, *An Humbler Heaven*, London, Hamish Hamilton, 1977, p. 2.

Combine this with his view of a decadent, faithless world, and a rigorous variety of pragmatism emerges, devoid of any of the illusions about the quality of our culture from which most of his underlings suffer.

You can waste a lot of time on generalizations. I think the only principle on which you can go is that the Arts Council will go on what the functions of the arts are which are natural to its time. The Arts Council is based on people who are close to the arts—it's the perception of mostly middle-aged people who've been close to the arts in the early 1980s. They're not going to be able to conduct a Platonic dialogue which will be of interest to people in two thousand years' time.

The wistful note is almost deafening: if only they *were* able! Sir William sees our age as unusually suffused with sin; the arts reflect the age. In his favourite century, the eighteenth, the idea of order and of reason produced the classical harmony for which he evidently yearns. It would be tempting to see in him the future, the new establishment of the arts in a transcendent context, the dream of Matthew Arnold, from which all else has since been falling away. In fact, Sir William is too much alone and his mission too institutionally based for him to impose an ideology on the industry. Besides, if he is far from the soft left, he is also far from the hard-right managerial class that discerns in the arts a macro-economic significance. Furthermore, the arts are not his primary interest. He speaks cogently and with characteristic fullness on the subject, but his ideas are conventional, lacking in involvement. On the subject of classical economics his voice rises perceptibly, and real thought comes tumbling out.

His key role is to provide an interruption in the liberal roll of honour. His reign is a hiatus in the intellectual growth of liberal arts funding, but its effects will be

largely benign. Practical results certainly ensue: the
decision to impose last year's 1 per cent cut on all
organizations rather than on a selection indicated a
version of the market economy for the subsidized
companies: they would have to sink or swim themselves.
There will also be a move towards the indigenous arts.
Sir William has said that he wants the literary tradition
to be celebrated.

What Sir William does not do, however, is provide an
answer to the question of what the arts actually do in a
wholly secular world. With some anxiety the Arts
Council has grasped the sense in which this needs to be
defined. Tony Field was therefore typically delighted
when Sir Isaiah Berlin responded to the Priestley
scrutiny with a sustained defence. Sir Isaiah is on the
board of Covent Garden, and characteristically Field had
been wanting to persuade one of that gathering of
heavyweights to produce a manifesto. The Berlin letter
to Priestley challenges the latter's assumption that the
Royal Opera House is 'above all an expression of national
will or identity'. This is the cosy formulation of the
defenders of the faith, who have not the nerve to abandon
the democratic context of liberal arts funding. Sir Isaiah
aims higher:

> My point is that advances in the arts in general and
> opera in particular are brought about by, at most,
> handfuls of individuals. I really do not think that 'the
> national will' plays any part in this sphere. When
> something marvellous is achieved—the ballet of
> Ashton, de Valois, Fonteyn; the acting of Olivier,
> Gielgud, Richardson, Edith Evans—it is a source of
> immense pride. These phenomena are not always
> founded on a native tradition, but on inspired efforts.

This defence is worth mentioning because it represents the truly mandarin position, the paternalistic

impulse to go ahead and do what is good, and one day the people will learn to agree with you. In reality it lies behind much of the liberal thinking but, of necessity, it is disguised by the egalitarian context. If given the chance, in Sir Isaiah's terms, the people may well vote against arts funding, but they will still thank God for Olivier.

I have concentrated in this chapter on the mandarins of the subsidized arts. Primarily this is because they are the ones who are obliged most directly to face the central issues. The commercial mandarins are first and foremost survivors—literary mullahs like Tom Maschler at Jonathan Cape or Christopher Sinclair-Stevenson at Hamish Hamilton, theatrical entrepreneurs like Ian Albery or Robert Fox, cinema ayatollahs like David Puttnam: all are applying their standards after the fact of having to make money. This may or may not produce better art, but in either case if it pays, it is justified.

What should be said is that it produces a greater degree of energy. The somewhat languid, weary air which surrounds so many of the subsidized mandarins will not be found among the commercial ones. The contrast between Puttnam's fluid chatter and Sir Peter Hall's smoke-wreathed meditations could not be greater. Nor could the electrified cynicism of Robert Fox and his partner Julian Seymour stand out more starkly against Sir Claus Moser's wistful idealism.

Yet the noise of the commercial sector and the languor of the subsidized are equally directionless. Both are playing markets founded on the one hand on money and, on the other, on some sort of critical consensus, which itself, according to the balance of subsidy argument, is obliged to find some sort of accommodation with hard cash. The contents of the shrine at which they all officiate remain as elusive as ever; perhaps they provide illumination, self-improvement or even mere culinary pleasures. But, whatever they do provide, the mandarin lives contentedly in the knowledge that they are there, infused with a quality known, for want of a better word, as art.

If one of these mandarins should be tipped as holding some sort of key to some sort of future, it is perhaps Sir Roy Strong. He has become chairman of an Arts Council panel. And with the Victoria and Albert Museum now running more or less along the lines he would like, 105 Piccadilly could be his next target—assuming, of course, that it remains a sufficiently substantial national body to allow him to have any impact, or to bother.

Sir Roy is a doer rather than a thinker. He speaks passionately about the lack of passion in others and bemoans the absence of any great men in this country any more. He wants, seemingly, endless razzmatazz— Arts Council award ceremonies, loud boasting about our achievements, less whingeing about money. For Sir Roy the arts are a curious combination of democratized style and good living. Quality is not so much defined as agreed upon; a downward curving and tightening of the lips is available to indicate the lack of it. He is at least alive, even if his recent escape into super-tastefulness with his new office decor and the deadly exhibition of the dress collection at the V&A hint that he may have a touch of the old malaise himself.

Sir Roy may be the future, not visionary but confident, not theoretical but stylish. A churchwarden at his local parish church, he also provides a neatly Anglican middle way between Sir William's icy Catholicism and the warm, muddy reefs of the soft left.

6

SOME ART

Today in the novel there is felt to have been a renaissance. Poetry is said to have found a new voice, painting a new spirit. Sculpture is addressing the world again rather than talking to itself. In the film world the British industry has seemingly been reborn, while theatre is perhaps just pausing before the next leap forward. On the matter of the next step in serious music the best opinions vary, rather as they do on the matter of the last. Interest in dance, however, has boomed.

All in all, the last five years have produced a distinct feeling that some corner has been turned, some new direction taken. Clearly, all these various rebirths cannot simply be compared. British cinema has risen primarily for economic reasons related to its association with an expanded television and video market. Poetry claims a genuine aesthetic renewal. Dance can be seen to have ridden a socio-aesthetic wave with as many inspirations from pop music and health fanaticism as from high art. Painting evidently needed to recover its equilibrium as the extreme innovations of the 1950s and 1960s had seemingly marked the end of the old days of easels, canvas and brushes.

They are all special cases, but they have one thing in common: they claim a return to old values of accessibility and direct relevance to the external world. *Gandhi* and *Chariots of Fire* are both poor films but both evidently appear solid, direct and meaningful in a way that commercial cinema seemed previously to have abandoned in an orgy of existential debates about whether the armed neighbourhood vigilante should gun down the black hood himself or call the police. Meanwhile the new enthusiasm for the English novel is marked by a significant number of 'well-made' books, honest, well-constructed brass-and-mahogany affairs like William Boyd's *A Good Man in Africa*. In poetry there is much excitement about narrative verse and a fascination with somewhat marginal trick effects.

And so on and so on. Art in the traditional, craft-based sense is back in fashion. The uneasy distance between artist and audience, in which once stood the dandy critic-mediator, has been bridged. This is a profound and complex development which, perhaps initially, can be linked with the rightward swing in politics. No-nonsense *petit bourgeois* economics finds its correlative, perhaps to the artists' discomfiture, in poems that tell stories or in films with a message. After all, extremism in art suggests the same kind of destabilization as extremism in politics.

A return to the centre is logical enough in the present climate. The strangely shaped edifice of the arts industry exists, so a continuation of the polarity between the safe, submissive old and the weird or cantankerous new could hardly be tolerated. Art could have gone one way and the arts another, but the latter cannot survive without constant reassurances that it embodies the former, so the gap had to be narrowed rather than gratuitously widened.

To this extent the development was an economic necessity. The industry at this stage of evolution could not abandon its customers. But there is also a deep, and not necessarily political, conservatism involved. This is generated by fear. The extent to which we felt threatened steadily increased through the 1970s. Nuclear war had somehow been dealt with until the sudden and relentless increase in tension after the invasion of Afghanistan. But the oil crisis indicated the fragility of our little world. It undermined the assumption that, while we had our ups and downs, the general trend was decidedly up. Conservation and environmentalism, both primarily anti-growth, conservative ideologies, became essential components of the average punter's intellectual baggage.

In this context the bleak pursuit of an increasingly rarefied modernist investigation of impotence was the last thing that was required. Tubular-steel chairs or randomly ordered novels reeked of the indulgent megalomania of growth. Cosy sofas and good reads do not. Perversely the expensive recreation of elaborate foreign operas also do not quite fit. They suggest waste, an anti-environmental tendency.

No. Art is now required to involve a certain generosity of intent—to grant its audience an escape, reassurance or confirmation of its views. This is an explicitly anti-modernist stance. The popular conception of modernism is that its experimental forms and compulsive extremity arose from something generally known as the 'modern world', an entity which drove sensitive souls to baffling distraction. This fits in neatly with the usual identification of art as a submissive mirror of the external or as sensitive reactor to current events. Anti- or post-modernism arises from a suspicious retreat from what has become perceived as modernism's over-reaction. Art is necessarily still seen as a mirror or reactor, but it must now operate through known forms and languages. The successful novel may now express impotence or terror before the shock of the new, but it must do so in the forms of a hundred years ago. Of course, under such conditions it can have only one possible message to deliver: that the abyss can be safely assimilated, that all manner of things shall be well.

The phrase 'post-modernism' was first popularized by

the architectural critic Charles Jencks, and architecture provides the most obvious demonstration of all of the scale of the retreat from modernism's icy Moscow. In architecture modernism meant the paring down of forms, the rejection of ornamentation, an emphasis on space rather than on surface and, as the logical conclusion of all these positions, the expression of structure: a building must appear to be precisely what it is. The most obvious result was the classic, slick, steel-and-glass office block. It seemed coherent, unchallengeable and entirely right. It conformed to economic demands and provided business with an image of unfussy efficiency. Over the years the form varied—emphasis was placed on horizontal rather than on vertical planes; the blocks were curved, twisted, coloured and extruded—yet they were still basically blocks. But throughout the principal concern was the purity of the solution, its integrity and its aspiration to stasis, the stillness of perfect form.

But it presupposed a heroic architect, a visionary with the will to impose his sensibility on the real world. There were two things wrong with this position. First, the appalling problems that modernist developments ran into. Environmentally and mechanically there was one disaster after another. The architect became the modern hate-figure. Second, most architects are neither heroes nor visionaries, and modernism is a dreadfully easy style to debase.

So along came post-modernism. Buildings were to be returned, accessible and fun, to the people who had always hated the skyscrapers anyway. Brick came back, even if it was only a facing rather than a structural element. (Only a modernist would worry about such things.) Arches, cornices and all the old hierarchy of architectural orders were made usable once again. The New Vernacular was born. It consisted of earnest attempts to use the traditional forms of housing as a basis for innovation rather than the discredited modernist forms. Pitched roofs came back along with elaborate windows, porches and deep, dark eaves. Architecture, said the post-modernists, is a language that people have spoken for years. The International Style of modernism was a gibberish interlude.

This is the last sentence of a note by the critic Vincent Scully on the work of the arch post-modernist Michael Graves: 'At one stroke, everything lost has returned, the monumental community building and its colossal figure sculpture: the human environment and the human act together.' The key here is the attempt to disguise the atavism of the intent. It is not the past which is being retreated to; something is being recovered that was lost. The International Style was a betrayal of something that we knew to be true all along. People were never interested in its formal absolutism; they wanted big statues and community buildings with meanings. That is what the post-modernists offered.

Unfortunately for Britain, two of its three internationally accepted architects are card-carrying modernists. Richard Rogers and Norman Foster are at the centre of the tradition, although they have added an emphasis on engineering which has earned them the usefully sanitized description of 'high-tech'. James Stirling, the third of the trio, has developed in more complex ways, clearly rejecting the mainstream of the ideology in his later work. It is ironic, however, that in one of the only arts in which we can boast international-standard artists, our own average quality has sunk spectacularly low. The deadly glueing-on of post-modernist styles in an attempt to 'pump up' bad buildings is perhaps the most comprehensive aesthetic disaster to hit London since the war.

Conveniently, all the architectural issues are to be

aired in the formal setting of a planning inquiry any day
now. Peter Palumbo, a property developer, wants to
build in the middle of the City of London an office block
and piazza designed by Mies van der Rohe. Palumbo is a
Mies fanatic and even possesses the door handles and
the ashtrays that the master has designed for his building. But he needs to knock down a block of Victorian
buildings (none of them distinguished) which forms,
according to the anti-Palumbo lobby, a unique fragment
of the old City which Hitler failed to destroy.

The other side of their case is more interesting for our
purposes. This is that the Mies building is itself old-
fashioned. Building it today would be like starting work
on another pyramid. And there can be no question that
the slick, clean lines of Mies' block do look old-fashioned
against the uncontrolled extravagances and incoherent
references of the post-modernist blocks that are defacing
the City. But, of course, the intellectual flaw in their
position is that by arguing thus they are espousing the
whole idea of a spirit of the age—that you can only build
in one way at any given time. It is precisely that
deterministic approach which the conservationists so
fervently attack elsewhere as being the mortal sin of
modern architecture.

But the real point is that Mies and his works are
identified with the period when, as Scully hints, everything was lost. The conservationists may well now
appeal to the spirit of the age because they are winning.
We are returning to an ill-defined past when architects
did not have Mies' unnerving confidence. Palumbo may
lose purely because of the prevailing feeling that
architects do not have the right to be geniuses any more.

A disgust with the present or the modern is nothing
new in the post-war years. The move to the right of the
Angry Young Men was accompanied by a certain nausea
provoked by the trappings of the contemporary world as

well as by a parochial rejection of nasty foreign developments. Similarly fashion and design, even in the heady sixties, brought with them a self-consciously backward glance. Terence Conran's spare interiors could always accommodate a hunk of Victorian cast iron or an old railway station sign. And, of course, the main role of organizations like the National Theatre or the Royal Opera House is to revive the past. New work is a relatively small proportion of their output.

But, throughout, the past has offered something more. It has offered stability and a system of codes and meanings which provide the illusion of an under-standable world. Scully's view of Graves is only slightly removed from gross sentimentality, possibly only a couple of pigeonholes away from the most characteristic popular cultural form of the 1970s and early 1980s: the television soap opera set in the past. From *Upstairs Downstairs* to *Brideshead Revisited* television laboured to produce 'real' worlds of moral certainty and aesthetic neutrality. True enough, this was show business providing what people appeared to want, but how easily the effect flooded upmarket! So the painstaking exactness of costumes and props, essential for the complete immersion of the viewer, is now to be found at the National. Similarly the whole fascination with old hierarchies, old pieties has been elevated to 'culture', as if the virtuous context of the word 'old' has spilled over from the antique dealer's vocabulary.

In architecture the *Upstairs Downstairs* era was marked by the growth of the conservation movement. If modern architecture was perceived as abysmal, the past should be preserved at all costs. If this meant stopping new developments, then so much the better. No age has ever shown such a preoccupation with the buildings of the past—though in fairness it should be added that no age has been subjected to so much redevelopment. Today all over London mediocre façades are being held up by steel girders while the rest of the building is knocked down and reborn as a disguised steel-and-glass block.

The effect of this obsession was a kind of monomania. The past was to be protected, recreated and cherished, sure enough, but soon it became *all* that was worth protecting. The future was evidently so malevolent and the immediate past so rabidly incompetent that the past (beginning at, say, 1939) was the only available experience of value.

Television as art, though necessarily a crude interpreter of the cultural climate, got this much dead right. The two BBC series based on John le Carré's books, *Smiley's People* and *Tinker, Tailor, Soldier, Spy*, portrayed old pre-war values and morals being pulverized by the requirements of latter-day *realpolitik*. It was all presented in a style lifted wearily from fragments of Dickens and flaunted as culture precisely because of its nostalgic impotence. In the new world you just have to stab your friend in the back with a wry, regretful, thoughtful smile, so let's dream about the old. It takes the sting away. Nothing could more potently catch the grim self-satisfaction of this vision than the credits that rolled over a shot of Oxford's dreaming spires as a choirboy sang in the background.

This and so many other products represented a crisis of confidence in the future which seemed to recapitulate the original crisis of modernism itself, with its perception of the failure of meaning and the primacy of form. But, in reality, it is a refusal of modernism, a turning away from its apocalyptic pioneering.

This reaction was implicit in the popular culture. It had always been a commonplace to point out that Dickens was a writer for the masses, and he was culturally OK. So what did these conceptualists and minimalists think they were up to? But the attitude had failed to gain fashionable acceptance. In smart circles it was hardly done to admit you were baffled, and there were always the Sunday newspapers to keep you afloat. But leisure journalism had produced only armchair connoisseurs who would have found, if they ever made it to the gallery or the theatre, that the reviews were better than the product itself. Reading a critic on an Abstract Expressionist painting or a Beckett play might, if you were not prepared, prove more illuminating than either. Significantly, it was Michael Graves who, in one of his more historically attuned remarks, said that criticism of American colour field painting—a form which had tended towards the blandest of abstractions—was more interesting than the paintings themselves. He had spotted the extent to which explanation had taken over from speculation, the word from the event.

There was a serious side to this development. Language had indeed become the centre of a substantial body of aesthetic thought in all forms, from poetry to painting. But the way in which the mandarin critics were using it to shift the focus from the art to themselves could produce only suspicion. A species of mistrust was born among the wanderers in the blizzard. A cocky philistinism gradually became respectable, isolating the avant-garde not only with a tiny actual audience but also with a nonexistent implicit audience.

This change in spirit has many implications. It represents a move away from art as a highly specialized, usually remote activity towards art in a new partnership with its audience. For the full before-and-after effect I shall use two quotations from the catalogues of major London exhibitions, both representing primary statements by the Culture Club about the nature of art at certain moments in history. The first is from the Tate Gallery catalogue of the 1971 Andy Warhol exhibition:

To depict Marilyn's lips 168 times in 49 square feet
is a more remarkable innovation than may first
appear. Requiring selection, masking, processing,
enlargement, transposition and application, in con-
junction with decisions on canvas size, placing colour
and handling, it means that the finished painting is a
complex and calculated artefact, which is not only
unique but strikingly different from any that another
individual might have produced. This truth, though so
startling a picture may make it more obvious, applies
equally to those of Warhol's works most maligned for
their failure to transform their source material or to
create anew. Though frequent dismissal of Warhol's
work as unoriginal on the ground that he is not
making new images is inherently absurd, since image-
invention is but one aspect of a work's potential
significance, ironically he is, in this very area,
creating with remarkable freshness.*

Precise analysis of all the elements in this dense,
polemical passage would take several volumes and
require considerable research into the history of certain
branches of aesthetics. But some points are clear. First,
the writer (Richard Morphet) is evidently impatient
with others' experience of Warhol's work. His is a
defensive position based on an admiration of the work
and an implicit belief in its importance. Second, the real
significance of his impatience is the way in which it
draws attention to the inadequacy of any response in the
conventional sense. Morphet emphasizes the primacy of
the artist's selective role *for itself*, not for the exterior
motive of creating responses in us. The anti-modernist
would reply that of course Warhol's pictures are subject
to all those processes of decision, but so were Constable's,

*Richard Morphet, 'Andy Warhol' exhibition catalogue, London, Tate
Gallery, 1971, p. 17.

and he gave us more than soup cans. But for Morphet the work stands unchallengeable, remote, preoccupied with the nature of its own form, abstracted from human considerations. Clearly, the realm of the picture has been invaded by language, but that is the fate of the object in a world apprehended via an inquiry into form—language being the ultimate form.

Next comes an extract from the catalogue of 'The Sculpture Show' at the Hayward and Serpentine Galleries in 1983:

Art of today is a consequence of a crisis of confidence in the rationalism of the classical episteme and has led to a renewal of faith in the irrational, imaginative and intuitive faculties of the spirit. In art it means a shift from the analytical and logical which determines the severity of minimal and conceptual art to the subjective, symbolic and archetypical. This resulted in a new passion for culture distant in space and time, archaic and crude forms, trivial art, prehistoric artefact and archeological remains. On the other hand the artist is well aware of his post-industrial economic environment and its unlimited possibilities for the assimilation, deposit and retrieval of images. The fact that we live in a new age of image sanctification in which the world becomes an interplay of signs that demand to be read and deciphered has caused a shift of focus in sculpture from object to image, from the thing itself to its appearance.*

Again the tone is polemical, but note the context. No longer are we amidst the minutiae of Warhol's silk-screen technology. Now we are dealing with classicism, the irrational, remote cultures and the electronic age.

*Nena Dimitrijevic, 'Sculpture and its Double: towards a Definition of Post-Evolutionary Sculpture', programme for 'The Sculpture Show', London, Arts Council of Great Britain, 1983, p. 138.

What this passage says, in a language carefully constructed to conform to the standards expected of Arts Council catalogues, is that art must mean something again, pictures must tell a story. The last sentence calls for a return to sculpture that *looks like* something rather than *is* something.

But, just like all the post-modernists, the writer (Nena Dimitrijevic) wants it both ways. She wants to appeal to a past before bleak modernism, and yet she does not want to forfeit the up-to-the-minute mirror/reactor role of art. This she accomplishes with the mix 'n' match phraseology of the all-purpose, bottomless coffee pot variety: 'Post-industrial economic environment' and 'the assimilation, deposit and retrieval of images'.

It is difficult to know which is worse—Morphet and his fastidious purity or Dimitrijevic and her ready-for-anything cultural baggage. But what matters is the change from art as thing-in-itself to art as the fruit in the muesli. In the first case it is a discernibly different experience, a package of effects obliged only to be true to themselves and scornful of the demands of the weakest members of its audience. In the second it is part of the whole, a fact in history.

Elsewhere, in poetry, Blake Morrison and Andrew Motion edited the *Penguin Book of Contemporary British Poetry* with the specific aim of identifying a new direction which, broadly, fits into the transition noted above. The book went to some lengths to establish how different it was from previous collections which had attempted similar feats of generalization: 'Now, after a spell of lethargy, British poetry is once again undergoing a transition.' The 'once again' is presumably bereft of ironical overtones to all but the most jaundiced of readers, who insisted on being appalled by the thoroughly marginal and backward-looking quality of most of what followed.

So the distrust of the modern and of the future, apparent for many years in popular culture, has spread to the respectable end of the market. It is disguised in all cases as a new direction and presented as refreshing, outgoing, free and accessible. Art is no longer to be driven by absolutes; it is to meet the audience halfway with poems that see familiar objects in a new light or with sculpture with both prehistoric and electronic overtones. It is an oddly pessimistic art, which accepts its fate of being plugged forever into the economic, social and historical exigencies of its age. Once again instant reaction, sensitivity to nothing more than newspaper headlines, is to be its authentication.

On the one hand this results in a return of art to a more stable view of its audience as consumers of a slowly evolving expressive system, and on the other it betrays the now familiar mistrust of planning, holistic thinking or, indeed, vision.

In 1983 the Greater London Council appointed Cedric Price, the radical modernist architect, to study the problems of London's South Bank arts complex. They were problems which, for most people, seemed to have arisen from the shortcomings of modern architecture itself. For them Price was hardly the man. Indeed, no architect could be. We had had enough of architects and their bright ideas. People could do it better. Simon Jenkins, journalist and leading conservationist, suggested that the way to solve the problems of the South Bank was to relax all planning controls, to allow small traders to spring up more or less uncontrolled, to let capitalism in the market place determine the South Bank's future. Architects, artists, visionaries, gurus, aesthete ninnies—what did they have to offer when confronted by the impersonal magic of the market place?

So the age of the hero has gone. Instead of madmen in pursuit of a formal absolute, we have to be content with

dinky fire stations with cute witches' hats in
Shaftesbury Avenue. Instead of Ezra Pound redefining
civilization we get verse parlour games. And so on and so
on. Only in drama is the big view alive and well, and
there it is condemned to the permanent limitation of a
political polemic.

But there is no question that there is a real
redefinition going on. In one sense it is a return to art as
a specific function in a specific context of specific
individuals at a specific distance from society. In a film
like *The Ploughman's Lunch* this sureness of context
becomes apparent, and the almost unanimously positive
critical reponse demonstrates the existence of the
market. The film was a simple attempt to talk to people
in newspaper headlines, to accept a realism undermined
only by a political perception. The motive for the title
itself—it was inspired by the insight that a plate of
bread, cheese and pickle was only named thus by an
advertising agency anxious to push pub food—suggests
the patronizing, didactic impulse which alone animates
the drab ciphers that limp through Ian McEwan's
lugubrious anxiety.

But the fact that the film was trite and unconvincing is
less important than the response of the critics. Scarcely a
single review questioned its masterly qualities, its
brilliant parallel between Suez and the Falklands War
as a revelation of our national moral and political
decline. But what the critics really relished was
something to write about. Here was a film that spoke
their language, the language of the middle-class saloon
bar in which opinions are validated by gross
generalizations and ill-researched historical parallels. It
was a film which suggested dozens of headings for
conversations (what we remember of Suez, or why
Jonathan Pryce looked at his watch in the last shot),
even if it was glaringly obvious that the overwrought,

downbeat significance of it was enough to send the sensitive screaming out of the cinema. Such a film returns art to its place as time killed, an instructive interlude. It drags art back from the frontiers it once shared with other disciplines precisely because those frontiers seemed to be leading to an inhuman desert or nowhere. It takes the pressure off the critics. They no longer have to be surrogate geniuses mediating between the audience and unacceptable works. By hedging every judgement, by avoiding a consistent view, they can relax and make sure they do not miss the next Cézanne, Buñuel or Joyce.

On the basis of such works it may seem clear that this phase is an aberration. They simply do not compete for lasting critical attention. Yet the critical surge of enthusiasm tells us a great deal about their context and, in the case of films, reveals a certain fatigue with the American moralist tradition and with the foreign 'art' movie syndrome. American films, of course, lost their innocence some time ago, when the French *Cahiers* critics and then the structuralists got hold of them, requiring them to be taken apart very seriously indeed. 'Art' movies, in contrast, had always represented a sort of dissent from the mainstream of popular films. With the monopoly distribution chains in this country they effectively demonstrated a formalized desire to preserve the gulf between mass civilization and minority culture. But *The Ploughman's Lunch* was neither American nor Continental and provided a novel sensation: the British and their problems seemed important. The lack of a British film industry had done more than throw people out of work; it had created the popular illusion that only in the past and in pastiche could we possibly have anything interesting to offer the world. The power of American iconography, created when we had nothing to offer in return, shook our imaginative confidence.

This newly assured parochialism in film matches similar movements elsewhere. It reveals a new distrust with the foreign, an aesthetic xenophobia which was the real root of Sir Claus Moser's bafflement when he noticed the critics preferring Harrison Birtwistle's austere Drill Hall production to the velvet glories of Covent Garden. We, the critics were saying, don't need all these trappings to experience the full artistic buzz. Small, private, sincere but intensely significant moments are where it's at. Remember the RSC's pride in stressing the little private jokes with its audience in which the Company indulges? Recognition is all, and certainly it must be comforting. For all *The Ploughman's Lunch*'s attempts to disturb, it offered only an argument, not a realization.

But again we return to the sense of withdrawal, the movement away from the modern to a submissive retrenchment of form. Malcolm Bradbury has pointed out the massive retreat of the novel in immediately post-war Britain—he cited the very title of Kingsley Amis's *I Like It Here* as a slightly creepy example of the old (or perhaps new) parochialism. He sees the new renaissance of the novel as evidence that modernism has at last penetrated the literary consciousness in this country. But this view appears to pay attention only to the fact of formal experiment rather than to its quality. In addition, of course, much of the renaissance is based on aggressively traditional fiction.

The key to all this lies, first, in the debatable area of what we call 'art' and, second, in what we want it to do. David Lodge wrote in an essay entitled 'The Novelist at the Crossroads':

The realist—and liberal—answer to this case must be that while many aspects of contemporary experience encourage an extreme, apocalyptic response, most of

us continue to live most of our lives on the assumption
that the reality which realism imitates actually exists.
History may be, in a philosophical sense, a fiction, but
it does not feel like that when we miss a train or
somebody starts a war.*

In other words, the apocalyptic extremity and
philosophical acceptance of fiction which characterized
modernism are found by the humanist to have a
profound shortcoming when confronted with 'real' life.
Only the facts of wars or missed trains can provide a
general human context for art. Riotous Dada behaviour
or cerebral attenuations of form are as nothing compared
with these great commonplace facts of human experience.

At this point nobody can remain seated on the fence
beyond saying that both sides can produce good stuff.
The value of individual achievement is not degraded by
the quality of a general movement. Where the choice
must lie is between the belief that the aesthetic
innovations of this century were as unavoidable as the
Romantic movement was in the last and the belief that
they were nothing more than a squalid hiatus and we are
just now getting back on the right lines.

The problem with modernism, of course, was that it
gave no easy answer to the question of what the
significance of the arts in the world was. The problem
with the reaction is that it evidently represents a return
to littleness, a retreat from the sense of the imagination
at the farthest reaches of its capability. It is, all too
clearly, compromised. Weakly Denis Donoghue, in his
1982 Reith Lectures, attempted to draw from this
confrontation a new aesthetic based on art as mystery.
The intent was to preserve their apartness by preventing

*David Lodge, 'The Novelist at the Crossroads', London, Routledge &
Kegan Paul, 1971; reprinted in Bradbury, *The Novel Today*, p. 109.

them from being reduced to mere problems. Problems can be dealt with; mysteries have to be lived with. For Donoghue 'even in a world mostly secular, the arts can make a space for mystery.' He denies any direct link between his art and his religion, but the link is clear enough—indeed, it is confirmed by his need to bother with a denial. But his uneasiness is perhaps the point. In a secular world there are no transcendent values. Art in the British tradition has always lived by its appeal to transcendent values. Admittedly, these have often seemed like the glorification of a purely defensive institutional position; nevertheless, it has been clear that art has meant good or better and has referred to something above and beyond the daily drudgery.

Modernism may be seen as an attempt to reconstruct the world in the absence of God—hence its heroic flavour and the scale of its undertakings, from Joyce's *Finnegan's Wake* to the *Cantos* of Ezra Pound. Post-modernism says that in the attempt we have abandoned the audience, the common man who thrived on Dickens.

Of course, all such aesthetic categories have an air of unreality about them. On the one hand good work often appears from the 'wrong' category and, on the other, the best work creates its own categories. Yet within a large and highly incestuous arts industry, in which fashion is as potent a force for change as innovation, it is impossible to ignore the broad tendencies in which the mainstream of creativity is obliged to operate. It is these tendencies which, to a damaging extent, sanction the availability of the product.

Take, for example, the current extraordinary obsession with lists in the publishing industry. This has emerged from two sources—the sudden and unexpected publicity success of the Booker Prize and the activities of the Book Marketing Council. The case of the Booker is complex. It cannot simply be written off as a huge commercial hype because the sales of short-listed and winning novels are boosted on a scale which betrays a real enough demand for the product. It seems rather to be a case of the publishers finding the public which has been waiting for their attentions for some time.

The point becomes clearer if the type of novel it promotes is considered. Recent winners have been Salman Rushdie with a novel about the evolution of India since independence, Thomas Keneally with a factually based novel about the concentration camps, and J. M. Coetzee with a novel about South Africa. All share clear external frames of reference of which we are aware as contemporary events in the real world. They are definably 'big' events, and they are foreign events— that is, they make the English feel guilty about their own lack of 'big' issues. Add to that recipe an acceptable degree of literary innovation—that, after all, is what serious novels are for—and you have a potential Booker Prize winner. (Not, it should be added, that it would stand much chance in the much more serious and genuinely literary Whitbread prize.)

It is an irresistible marketing mix, and it discovered a hungry public which had for years been deprived of the cachet of literature. Its appetite initially took the publishers by surprise, though it has since been assimilated, and the Booker circus now seems to consist of a series of familiar *éminences grises* of the book world emerging annually to press the appropriate series of marketing buttons.

The obsession with the Booker book swings the market in the direction of those enormous sales. The sheer industrial momentum created by the vertiginous peaks on the sales graphs shifts the taste of editors and turns temporary fashions into irresistible bandwagons. But, the defence always goes, at least it brings money into literature. And this has been the inspiration of the

Book Marketing Council's drive to persuade publishers
to act in concert simply to sell more books. The BMC,
with quite extraordinary success, produced one list after
another—'Best of British', 'Best of Young British
Novelists' and so on—with the happy conviction that,
whatever happens, people will work up an anger. The
Council detected the simple and blindingly obvious fact
of commercial life that all publicity is good publicity.
So the wisecracking, world-weary attacks on the
interminable lists were all grist to the Book Marketing
Council's mill.

The BMC's systematic and roguish hypes were
relatively harmless compared with the dictatorial
pretensions of the Booker. Yet both reveal a hunger to be
told. The public wants literature, and it is desperate
for guidance about where to find it. It is a repeat
performance of the 1960s, but this time instead of the
critics and the Sunday newspapers there are panels of
judges or experts. It is a change that reflects the more
systematic, industrialized artistic climate but springs
from the same insecurity, the same need to believe in art
as communal intermediary.

So the categories of modernism, post-modernism or
whatever are not simply feeble aesthetic distinctions.
Now they tend to have real marketing muscle behind
them. Of course, the poor, oppressed genius, out of step
with his age, has always been a standard image of the
artist. He lives and dies unrecognized, only to live again
when his true worth is discovered, possibly centuries
later. The trouble with a climate in which fashion is
backed with ferocious determination by marketing is
that it tends to increase the likelihood that this will
happen. Works will necessarily be judged by the extent
to which they say and do the right things rather than by
the quality of their execution.

Of course, there is nothing wrong with giving the

public what it wants or even with telling the public what it wants and then providing it. In either case it is only a game. Unfortunately, it is a game which requires large claims to be made. The qualities of art and genius are needed to season the marketing mix. This is art, say the salesmen. It is good for you. You need it....

7

SOME HOPE

A light snow, like frost, has fallen during the night.
Gloomily, the journalist confronts

Transparent man in a translated world,
In which he feeds on a new known...

Wallace Stevens, 'On the Way to the Bus'

In the 1983 programme for the Glyndebourne Festival
Opera there is a full-page advertisement for Prudential
Pensions Limited of 142 Holborn Bars, London EC1N
2NH. 'Our performance', reads the caption, 'will bring
music to your ears.' Beneath is a picture of an elderly
man in a dinner jacket and a red cummerbund. He has
been caught in the act of enjoying the traditional
Glyndebourne supper interval. He sits on a wooden
bench decorated with carved bass and treble clefs. His
legs are outstretched and crossed at the ankle. On his lap
is an open copy of an opera score. His fingers are
interlaced behind his head which is flung back in an
attitude of beatific relaxation. The eyes are closed. His
moustache and hair are snowy-white—distinguished.
Beside him on the bench are his discarded spectacles and
a glass of wine. Beneath the bench is a half-open picnic
basket out of which a bottle of champagne coyly peeps.
The whole is painted in a distasteful, hyper-realistic
manner which takes some delight in rendering the
creases in the man's clothing and the texture of the
bushes behind. The skin appears tanned or possibly
reddened by high blood pressure.

Lewisham's Riverdale Shopping Centre is a fairly

typical modern mall. At its centre is an elaborate device
which, on the hour, plays a tune and reveals a series of
animated puppets of Cockney characters. In the space
below there is usually an exhibition of double-glazing or
a local photographer at work. On one quiet weekday
afternoon the Centre is filled by neither of these things.
Instead there are large, plain, white boards supporting
big canvases. They are paintings of a somewhat muddy
hue but clearly executed by somebody with a degree of
skill and knowledge of art history—there are fragments
of Picasso, Masson and Dali. They appear to be placed
there entirely without comment. Closer inspection
reveals a self-consciously small and modest typewritten
sheet announcing that the pictures were executed by some
local artist in residence. They are generally ignored,
though a brace of skinheads shows mild interest.

At the end of Alban Berg's opera *Lulu* the heroine and
her lesbian admirer Countess Geschwitz have both been
murdered by Jack the Ripper. They die on a grey,
rubbish-strewn set in Götz Friedrich's Royal Opera
House production, revived last year. Jack stands
silhouetted at the back of the stage in a pillar of white
created by the sudden splitting of the black backdrop. It
is a cold, heartless conclusion to a brilliant work of art—
a vision of the wilful desecration of mere subhumans at
the hands of a gratuitous plot, all imprisoned in a cold,
hard musical structure. In the programme notes on the
music Douglas Jarman remarks on the 'humanity and
pity which this great opera embodies'. As usual, Karan
Armstrong, who has sung Lulu, is presented with a
bouquet by the ROH's obligatory liveried flunkey during
the applause, which is warm even though many have left
before the end.

Rank Xerox is announcing a new arts sponsorship
venture at a lunch for journalists and Lord Gowrie, the
Minister for the Arts. The Minister is very keen to

encourage as much commercial sponsorship as possible, so he tends to be rather startlingly available on these occasions. At the end he speaks of 'a very agreeable lunch in enlightened company who are not asking for money'.

The arts world is an old chaos of misunderstandings, tentative connections, obligations and associations. In those senses it is like any other human world. Doubtless a catalogue of the ideas which animate the aerospace or textile industries would reveal equally elaborate and inconsistent structures. But one element singles out the arts as a distinctly curious sector of the national life— the slender, fragile and shifting idea of art itself. Balancing on this tiny point is the upturned pyramid that I have been describing.

In my first chapter I raised the possibility that the very word 'art' was now in danger of becoming defunct. And, given the general climate of opinion which believes we are about to leave the phase of our development begun by the industrial revolution, that would be a neatly logical development. As Raymond Williams has pointed out in *Culture and Society*, it was in the late eighteenth and early nineteenth centuries that the modern connotations of the word were born—in other words, at the same time as the first signs of widespread industrialization. 'Art' moved away from being any human skill to being one particular kind of skill in the fields of literature, music, painting or sculpture. These activities were seen as sharing an aspiration to imaginative truth and to the condition of art, a condition over and above anything defined solely by talent or craft.

That movement immediately implies a *difference* between art and other human activity. It is an indefinable difference and is therefore open to any amount of abuse. Its existence as a potent and active idea has meant that art has been obliged to accept the burden of any number of associations and requirements in order to provide evident and provable justification for its unnerving *difference*. In a primarily religious society its power was linked with that of divine revelation. In a secular one it is said to do people good with varying degrees of intensity.

In all cases the associations cast light only on those who would convince us. They demonstrate, usually, the need to believe that an intense, private experience must have a wider application, must have a place in a religious hierarchy or a secular strategy for the improvement of mankind's lot. Sometimes they merely demonstrate crude self-interest—the protection of an institution or the freedom to indulge a taste.

With improved education and prosperity, as well as the more rapid means of transmission of information, the rate at which these human needs are suspended from the fragile notion of art has accelerated. Wild distortions have occurred. Strange creatures with orange hair wander through the opening parties for new exhibitions. They greet each other by touching cheeks and kissing the air. Novelists feel qualified to pass judgement on the political future of their countries on the basis of a slender talent for extended prose narrative. All are endorsed by the freedom of creativity, the *difference* of art.

The need to believe that art somehow bears all these things within it has produced the strange beast I have been trying to describe. Attempts to demystify the arts have often been made, but it remains clear that without this sense of difference, of some wider significance, the energies that animate the creature would long ago have been dissipated. The past, the new arts, the money, the mandarins and the state of art today are all aspects of one complex legacy, one wild, rococo elaboration on thousands of disparate moments of private intensity.

Of course, the most obvious and definitive statement

that this intensity has external responsibilities and implications is subsidy. Virtually all the arts are now subsidized—the performing arts most obviously, but also literature, primarily by libraries. That leaves only cinema still for the most part directly answerable to demand. The politics of subsidy have meant that art has been required to be different things in different environments. For Labour and the old Tories it was a welfare benefit. For the New Right it is a significant industry. The latter definition takes art out of the realm of the Romantic, visionary tradition and into a new, possibly more objective, territory. It may finally provide a more stable climate in which, although artists may still feel obliged to fight, they will do so in the knowledge that their enemy's logic has a gratifying consistency.

Yet this says nothing about the great paradox of modern art. For while all this paraphernalia of association has been dragged into the idea of art, art itself has been systematically turning in on itself, proclaiming its authenticity by flaunting its self-containedness, its integrity only to itself.

'His writing is not *about* something,' shrieked Samuel Beckett at James Joyce's detractors, *'it is that something itself.'* That, of course, is the logical conclusion of the Romantic statement that art was different. Having failed to be different for religious or social reasons, it has become different because of the one quality it appears to share with nothing else—its self-referring, useless completeness. However futile this may sound, it is not a dead end. There are great artists working today who have taken up the challenge, and great ones will follow them.

How this self-involved, self-conscious art relates to the arts is a problem. For that in reality is where 'art'—defined as the highest attainments of the human imagination—now stands. It is not immediately obvious how that can come to terms with street theatres, craft workshops, Covent Garden or the National Theatre—how, in a word, it can continue to support them.

The gap between the term 'art' as applied to, say, the painting of Mondrian and as applied to street theatre has been created by the rapid fragmentation and expansion of the industry. It may be argued that this is merely a verbal point, but it does produce genuine practical difficulties. In the finest and most blissfully squeamish passage from the Select Committee's report on arts funding, the problem of definition is raised. It takes the overall view that there is no point in limiting the task in hand, so no definition is really necessary. The MPs did, however, look into several possibilities as to the 'true meaning of art'. There was, for example, Dr Richard Hoggart's view that the arts are 'essentially about the exploration of values and criticism of other people's values and of society'. Then there was the Minister, who believed that the arts should just provide pleasure and 'sometimes learning'. Well, up to a point, but the Committee finally found it best to stick with the definition provided by Mr Kenneth Robinson, then chairman of the Arts Council, who said that the arts were a 'multifarious affair'. From this the Committee derived the implication that content is best left to artists, clients and audiences 'to decide upon between themselves'.

This level of dilution has laid the foundations of a clearer identification of the arts as a major industry. Evidently it is impossible to sustain an industry which keeps quibbling about the right word for its product, so all options should be kept open. The Committee's vagueness has prepared the way for a breakdown of the divisions, in so far as they still exist, between arts and entertainment, arts and leisure—divisions which to a large extent have already been undermined by the

listings magazines, the leisure sections of the newspapers and the general slap-happiness of the 1960s and
after.

Once these divisions have been broken down, of
course, we will be ready for the leisure revolution which
is coming our way, thanks to microprocessors and their
offspring. Optimists say that this will lead to a massive
increase in the number of customers for the arts and that
now is the time to invest. Pessimists claim that it will
lead to a massive increase in the number of video nasties
and little else. But once the arts start being a single,
cohesive industry it will hardly matter. Video nasties
will be as much part of the new statistically defined arts
as the English National Opera. They will both come
under some global figure of around £3,000 million.

At that point it would become convenient, indeed
necessary, to suppress the whole idea of difference.
Distinction would come to be based more on marketing
considerations and on the advertising man's socio-
demographic analyses. The As and Bs would, of course,
continue to cling on to their qualitatively superior
entertainment, but the notion of excellence would have
lost its structural function within the industry. And
there is the neatness of the idea of art being drained of
meaning. The word was created in its modern context at
the time of the industrial revolution; just as we enter the
so-called post-industrial society, it is becoming defunct.

If this analysis and the preceding survey seem unduly
negative, then they are perhaps only a response to a
distinctly forced air of glee and complacency within the
arts. I am not denying that good and occasionally great
things have been done. I am saying that in a period
of cultural decline a strange, sick determination has
developed to make creativity do and be something—to
make it obligatory. Frank O'Hara, a fine American poet,

has provided the healthiest response to this attitude:

> But how can you really care if anybody gets it, or gets
> what it means, or if it improves them? Improves them
> for what? For death? Why hurry them along? Too
> many poets act like a middle-aged mother trying to get
> her kids to eat too much cooked meat and potatoes
> with dripping (tears). I don't give a damn whether they
> eat or not. Forced feeding leads to excessive thinness
> (effete). Nobody should experience anything they don't
> need to; if they don't need poetry, bully for them. I like
> the movies too.*

Perhaps the loss of any meaning at all in art would
clear the ground for the kind of freedom that O'Hara
offers. Perhaps the inclusion of the drop of art in the
ocean of leisure would release it from its accreted
obligations. New words might help. We could, say, label
'Alpha' the poems of John Ashbery, the prose of Beckett
and the films of Andrei Tarkovsky, and the rest 'Beta'
and 'Gamma' and so on. This would at least imply
a hierarchy without external reference, potentially
freeing the genuinely great from the unwelcome
attentions of relevance, value or industrial significance.
But then somebody would probably come along and say
that the 'Alpha'-producers were the unacknowledged
legislators of the world. . . .

*Frank O'Hara, 'Personism: a Manifesto', *Yūgen 7*, 1961; reprinted in
The Collected Poems of Frank O'Hara, ed. Donald Allan, New York,
Alfred A. Knopf, Inc., 1971, p. 498.

INDEX